REQUEST FORM

LITERATURE
P R E N T I C E   H A L L

Reader's Companion Audio Programs

The *Prentice Hall Literature Reader's Companion Audio Programs* provide professional recordings of all the literature selections in the Reader's Companion, Reader's Companion Adapted Version, and Reader's Companion English Learner's Version. These audio companions help build fluency through listening skills and allow you to customize your teaching to meet your students' needs.

To order audio CDs free of charge:

1. Complete the form below, and mail it postage-paid to the address indicated on the reverse side.

OR

2. FAX your request to 1-614-771-7365. If you wish to receive confirmation of your order, please include your fax number.

MAIL THIS CARD FREE   OR   FAX TO 1-614-771-7365

Please send me the item checked below to accompany my *Prentice Hall Literature: Timeless Voices, Timeless Themes* Reader's Companions. (Select one.)

Reader's Companion Audio CDs	Adapted and English Learner's Audio CDs
__ Grade 6 0-13-180336-0	__ Grade 6 0-13-180329-8
__ Grade 7 0-13-180337-9	__ Grade 7 0-13-180330-1
__ Grade 8 0-13-180338-7	__ Grade 8 0-13-180331-X
__ Grade 9 0-13-180339-5	__ Grade 9 0-13-180333-6
__ Grade 10 0-13-180341-7	__ Grade 10 0-13-180344-1
__ Grade 11 0-13-180342-5	__ Grade 11 0-13-180334-4
__ Grade 12 0-13-180343-3	__ Grade 12 0-13-180335-2

SHIP TO: (Please print clearly)

School:_____

Attention:_____

School Address:_____

City:_____ S

School Phone: (_ _ _) _ _ _-_ _ _ _

School Fax: (_ _ _) _ _ _ -_ _ _ _

(Include Fax number for confirmation)

D1529914

PRENTICE HALL
PO Box 2500
Lebanon, IN 46052-9924

First Clas
U.S. Pos
PAID
Permit #
S. Hackens

BUSINESS REPLY MAIL

FIRST-CLASS   PERMIT NO. 102   LEBANON, IN

POSTAGE WILL BE PAID BY ADDRESSEE

PRENTICE HALL

PO Box 2500
Lebanon, IN 46052-9929

NO POSTA
NECESSA
IF MAILE
IN THE
UNITED STA

PRENTICE HALL
LITERATURE

Reader's
COMPANION
TEACHING GUIDE

Bronze Level

PEARSON

Prentice
Hall

Upper Saddle River, New Jersey
Needham, Massachusetts

Pearson Prentice Hall™ is a registered trademark of Pearson Education, Inc.

Pearson® is a registered trademark of Pearson plc.

Prentice Hall® is a registered trademark of Pearson Education, Inc.

ISBN 0-13-180304-2

2 3 4 5 6 7 8 9 10   07 06 05 04

© Pearson Education, In

Contents

Reader's Companion

Reader's Companion Adapted Version

Reader's Companion English Learner's Version

How to Use the *Reader's Companions*

Share the same selection with all your students!

STEP 1

Introduce instruction using *Prentice Hall Literature* Student Edition

- Use the Background information
- Introduce the Literary Analysis and Reading Strategy
- Preview the vocabulary words

STEP 2

Develop instruction with targeted reading support

Choose the *Reader's Companion* that meets each student's needs

Reader's Companion
- For average readers
- Full-length selections with interactive reading support
- Vocabulary and pronunciation guides
- All selections on audio CD

Adapted Version
- For struggling readers
- Selection adaptations and authentic text
- Enhanced design for easier readability
- All adapted selections on audio CD

English Learner's Version
- Specialized vocabulary and reading support
- Focus on idioms, colloquialisms, and cultural information
- All adapted selections on audio CD

STEP 3

Conclude instruction using *Prentice Hall Literature* Student Edition

- Present the unabridged selection and instruction in the student edition
- Have students read along with the audio CDs
- Use the scaffolded questions in Review and Assess

To the Teacher

As you face the challenge of heterogeneous classes, you will find a wide variety of abilities and strengths among your students. The *Reader's Companion*, the *Reader's Companion Adapted Version*, and the *Reader's Companion English Learner's Version* that accompany your *Prentice Hall Literature* anthology are aimed at students who have difficulty with their grade-level textbook. You can use the *Companions* to keep your classes reading the same selections but getting the instruction and reading support at the appropriate level. These books provide extended support for those students who need more guidance with reading strategies, literary analysis, and critical thinking skills.

Factors that Affect Reading Success

Four key factors influence students' ability to achieve reading success. These factors, alone and in combination, determine how well a student will learn, grow, and succeed as a reader. To understand the students in your classroom, consider these factors:

(a) **Kinds of Learners** Consider each student's background, previous learning experiences, and special needs. In addition to students who read fluently at grade level, you may find a mix of the following learning characteristics in your classroom:

- *Students who speak a language other than English at home* Unlike their fully fluent counterparts, these students often speak English only at school. This situation leaves them limited hours in which to learn the grammar, vocabulary, idioms, and other intricacies of English.

- *Students who have recently moved to this country* These students may be highly capable students without the specific language skills to function academically in English.

- *Students with learning disabilities* These students may have cognitive, behavioral, social, or physical challenges that make reading more difficult.

(b) **Kinds of Skills and Instruction** Students' reading ability is influenced by the skills they bring to the task. Students must master the skills of decoding, activating, and building prior knowledge and making connections among experiences and new information. Other factors include a student's knowledge of the English language and vocabulary and a student's ability to apply reading comprehension strategies.

Active reading, including the practice of summarizing, questioning, setting a purpose, and self-monitoring, is key to successful reading. For those students who have not yet developed such skills, your classroom instruction is critical. You should model such skills and encourage students to practice them. Through practice, students should be able to internalize the strategies of active reading.

(c) **Kinds of Texts** Just as students and their backgrounds and skills vary, so do the texts presented in a language arts curriculum. The grade-level language arts classroom curriculum traditionally addresses fiction, nonfiction, poetry, and drama. Each of these forms presents unique challenges to students. Each writer and selection also presents challenges in the difficulty of the concepts addressed or in the coherence of the writing. For example, you may find that students are more comfortable with narratives than with expository writing. Focused reading strategies that you model and reinforce can help students tackle texts that are more dense or difficult for them to master.

(d) **Classroom Environment** The classroom environment affects everything and everyone within it. Research suggests that students learn best in a friendly, respectful setting categorized by these criteria:

- Students feel a sense of safety and order.
- They feel comfortable taking risks.
- They understand the purpose and value of the tasks presented.
- They have high expectations and goals for learning.
- They feel accepted by their teachers and peers.

Students performing below grade level may be especially self-conscious. Therefore, these criteria are key to helping students take full advantage of the opportunities the classroom affords. Set up your classroom as a caring yet on-purpose environment that helps students achieve.

Researchers encourage teachers to be truthful with students about the work it will take to build and master abilities in the language arts. Tell your students that improving reading, writing, speaking, and listening takes a great deal of practice. You need to be prepared to provide direct instruction, guided practice, specific feedback, coaching, and more. Then, encourage your students to understand their responsibilities as active, self-directed learners as well.

The Special Education or Special Needs Student

Your classroom may have a number of special education or special needs students—young people who begin the year three or more years below grade level and yet do not qualify for special education services. Special education and special needs students have difficulty in organizing and categorizing new information during instruction. They may have trouble in the following areas:

Memory

- ordering or arranging information

- classifying information

- grasping a main idea or "big picture"

- using long-term memory to make meaningful connections or connecting to prior knowledge

Attention

- focusing attention on the most important elements of a presentation or a selection

By presenting specific focused strategies and interactive review and extension activities, you can provide these students with full access to the language arts curriculum.

Another category of deficiency in special education readers is the ability to apply learning strategies to a variety of situations. Special education and special needs students often have these weaknesses:

Learning Strategies

- a lack of effective or efficient strategies for completing academic tasks such as taking notes, responding to literature, or writing a focused paragraph

- a limited set of learning strategies from which to draw

- difficulty in self-monitoring—they often don't know which strategies to use or when a strategy is not working

Many of these students are underprepared; their deficiencies are generally based on their lack of experience, not on any biological difference. When these students learn effective strategies, they can improve their academic performance. You need to provide direct instruction to explicitly show them how, when, and why to use each strategy.

Overview of Components for Universal Access

The *Prentice Hall Literature: Timeless Voices, Timeless Themes* program includes an array of products to provide universal access. Fully integrated, these materials help teachers identify student needs or deficiencies, teach to the varying levels in a classroom, and provide the quality that literature teachers expect.

As your main resource, the *Annotated Teacher's Edition* provides a lesson plan for every selection or selection grouping. In addition to teaching notes and suggestions, the *Annotated Teacher's Edition* also includes cross-references to ancillary material such as the *Reader's Companion*, the *Reader's Companion Adapted Version*, and the *Reader's Companion English Learner's Version*. Customize for Universal Access notes help teachers direct lessons to the following groups of students: special needs students, less proficient readers, English learners, gifted and talented students, and advanced readers.

The **Teaching Guidebook for Universal Access** gives you proven strategies for providing universal access to all students. In addition to its general teaching strategies and classroom management techniques, this component explains how the parts of the Prentice Hall program work together to ensure reading success for all student populations.

The **Reading Diagnostic and Improvement Plan**—part of the Reading Achievement System— provides comprehensive diagnostic tests that assess students' mastery of reading skills. The book also includes charts that help you map out an improvement plan based on students' performance on the diagnostics.

You can use the **Basic Reading Skill: Comprehensive Lessons for Improvement Plan**—also part of the Reading Achievement System— to give instruction and practice that bring students up to grade level, enabling them to master the skills in which they are deficient. For each skill covered, you'll find the following materials:

- lesson plan with direct instruction

- teaching transparency

- blackline master for student application and practice

The **Reader's Companion** is a consumable component of the Reading Achievement System. The book contains the full text of approximately half of the selections from the student book. Questions prompt students to interact with the text by circling, underlining, or marking key details. Write-on lines in the margins also allow for students to answer questions. You can use this book in place of the student book to help students read interactively.

The **Reader's Companion Adapted Version** is another consumable component of the Reading Achievement System. This book uses the same format and contains the same selections as the *Reader's Companion*. However, the selections are abridged and appear in a larger font size. The questions are targeted toward special education students. You can use this book as a supplement to or in place of the student book for certain selections to enable special education students to experience the same literature and master the same skills as on-level students.

The **Reader's Companion English Learner's Version** is a third consumable component of the Reading Achievement System. This book uses the same format and contains the same selections as the *Reader's Companion*. Again, the selections are abridged and appear in a larger font size. The questions are targeted toward English learners. You can use this book as a supplement to or in place of the student book for certain selections to enable English learners to experience the same literature and master the same skills as students who are native English speakers.

Reader's Companion Audio Program These components feature professional recordings of every selection in the *Reader's Companion*. To support student reading, you can play the selections, in part or in full, before students read them.

Reader's Companion Adapted and English Learner's Version Audio Program These components feature professional recordings of every adapted selection in the *Adapted Reader's Companion* and *English Learner's Companion*. The recordings include the explanatory bridges along with the lines of original text. As with the *Reader's Companion* audio components, you can support student reading by playing selections, in part or in full, before students read them.

The *Reader's Companion Audio Program* and the *Reader's Companion Adapted and English Learner's Version Audio Program* can be used to support reading fluency. As you play the CDs, have students read along, either silently or aloud.

Spanish/English Summaries Audio CD Audio summaries in both English and Spanish are provided for every selection. You can play these selection summaries for struggling readers, special education students, and English learners before they read the actual texts.

Basic Language Skills: Reteaching Masters With the reteaching masters, you can provide basic-level instruction and practice on grammar and language skills.

Interest Grabber Videos These videos are an optional enrichment resource designed to provide background for a selection or otherwise motivate students to read the selection. There is a video segment for every selection or selection grouping in the student book.

About the *Reader's Companion Adapted Version* and the *Reader's Companion English Learner's Version*

The *Reader's Companion Adapted Version* and the *Reader's Companion English Learner's Version* are designed to support your special education and special needs students.

Part 1: Selection Adaptations with Excerpts of Authentic Text

Part 1 will guide special needs students and English learner's as they interact with half the selections from *Prentice Hall Literature: Timeless Voices, Timeless Themes.* This range of selections includes the more challenging selections, the most frequently taught selections, and many examples of narrative and expository writing. Part 1 provides pre-reading instruction, larger print summaries of literature selections with passages from the selection, and post-reading questions and activities.

The **Preview** page will help your students get the general idea of the selection and therefore be better equipped to understand it. Written and visual summaries, along with a photograph or illustration, preview the selections before students read the adapted versions.

The **Prepare to Read** page is based on its parallel in *Prentice Hall Literature: Timeless Voices, Timeless Themes.* It introduces the same literary element and reading strategy addressed in the textbook and provides a graphic organizer to make the information more accessible.

The **selection** pages present the text in a larger font size. Interspersed among blocks of authentic text, these *Companions* also provide summaries of episodes or paragraphs to make the selections more accessible to your students.

The **side notes** make active reading strategies explicit, asking students to look closely at the text to analyze it in a variety of ways. Notes with a *Mark the Text* icon prompt students to underline, circle, or otherwise note key words, phrases, or details in the selection. Notes with write-on lines offer students an opportunity to respond in the margin to questions or ideas. These notes offer focused support in a variety of areas:

Literary Analysis notes provide point-of-use instruction to reinforce the literary element introduced on the Preview page. By pointing out details or events in the text in which the literary element applies, these notes give students the opportunity to revisit and reinforce their understanding of literature.

Reading Strategy notes help students practice the skill introduced on the Preview page. These notes guide students to understand when, how, and why a strategy is helpful.

Stop to Reflect notes ask students to reflect on the selection or on a skill they are using. By encouraging students to solidify their own thinking, these notes help to develop active reading skills.

Reading Check notes help students confirm their comprehension of a selection. These notes help to make explicit a critical strategy of active reading.

Read Fluently notes provide students with concrete, limited practice reading passages aloud with fluency.

Background notes provide further explanation of a concept or detail to support students' understanding.

THESE INSTRUCTIONAL NOTES ARE SPECIFIC TO THE *READER'S COMPANION ENGLISH LEARNER'S VERSION*:

Vocabulary and Pronunciation notes guide students in understanding prefixes, suffixes, roots, and words with multiple meanings. In some cases, they explain how specific words are pronounced in English.

Culture Notes explain an aspect of American culture that might be unfamiliar to English Learners. They may focus on an aspect of popular culture or on an event or a concept of historical significance.

The *Review and Assess* questions following the selection ensure students' comprehension of the selection. Written in simple language, they assess students' understanding of the literary element and the reading strategy. In addition, they offer a scaffolded guide to support students in an extension activity based on either a writing or a listening and speaking activity in the *Student Edition* of the grade-level textbook.

Using the *Companions*

Classroom Management:

When you are planning lessons for heterogeneous classes, the *Companion Readers* offer you an opportunity to keep all the students in your class reading the same selection and studying the same vocabulary, literary element, and reading strategy but also to get the support they need to succeed. At the outset, assign appropriate *Companions* to the students and have them write their names in them. Students very quickly assume ownership as they complete the interactive format of the *Companions*. The books become a personalized "response journal" and study guide for tests as they move through the selections.

Here are some planning suggestions for using these books in tandem with the grade-level volume of *Prentice Hall Literature: Timeless Voices, Timeless Themes*:

Use the *Annotated Teacher's Edition* and the *Student Edition* of the grade-level textbook as the central text in your classroom. The *Annotated Teacher's Edition* includes *Customize for Universal Access* notes throughout each selection. In addition, it identifies when use of the *Companions* is appropriate.

Accountability:

Collect the *Companions* at intervals that you choose. For example, you may decide to review students' work in the *Companions* once weekly. Have students mark a page completed during that time period with a sticky note, which can be used as a tab. This tab makes it easy for you to open the *Companion* quickly to the specific page, check for the accuracy and thoroughness of the work on selected questions, and award points or a grade.

Absent students:

Use the *Reader's Companion* for students who will be absent during discussions or for home-bound students. These students will be in step with the rest of the class in terms of concepts, strategies, and standards covered during their absence.

Teaching Part One: The Selections

PRE-TEACH with the Full Class

Consider presenting the **Interest Grabber** *video segment.* This optional technology product can provide background and build motivation.

Preview the selection. To help students see the organization of a selection, or to help them get a general idea of the text, lead a quick text pre-reading or "text tour" using the textbook. Focus student attention on the selection title, the art accompanying the text, and any unusual text characteristics. To build connections for students, ask them to identify links between the selection and other works you have presented in class or to find connections to themes, activities, or other related concepts.

Build background. Use the Background information provided in the *Student Edition.* Whether explaining a historical time period, a scientific concept, or details about an idea that may be unfamiliar to students, this instruction presents useful information to help all students place the literature in context.

Focus vocabulary development. The *Student Edition* includes a list of vocabulary words included in the selection or selection grouping. Instead of attempting to cover all of the vocabulary words you anticipate your students will not know, identify the vocabulary that is most critical to talking and learning about the central concepts. However, for the words you do choose to teach, work to provide more than synonyms and definitions. Using the vocabulary notes in the *Annotated Teacher's Edition,* introduce the essential words in more meaningful contexts: for example, through simple sentences drawing on familiar issues, people, scenarios, and vocabulary. Guide students in internalizing the meanings of key terms through these familiar contexts and ask them to write the definitions in their own words. Look at the following examples of guided vocabulary instruction:

Point out the word *serene* and explain that it means "calm or peaceful." Then, provide the following scenarios and ask students to determine whether the situations are *serene* or not: an empty beach at sunset *(yes)*; a basketball playoff game *(no)*. You might also ask students to provide their own examples of *serene* situations.

Point out the word *interval* and explain that it means "the period of time between two events or points of time." Ask students to identify the interval between Monday and Wednesday *(two days)* and the interval between one Monday and the next Monday *(one week)*.

You might also take the opportunity to teach the prefix *inter-*, meaning "between." Then, discuss with students the following group of words:

interview (a meeting between two or more people);

interstate (between two or more states);

international (between nations);

intervene (to come between two sides in a dispute).

Introduce skills. Introduce the *Literary Analysis* and *Reading Strategy* using the instruction in the *Student Edition* and the teaching support in the *Annotated Teacher's Edition.*

Separate the class. As average level students begin reading the selection in the *Student Edition*, have struggling readers, special education students, special needs students, and English learners put their textbooks aside. Direct these students to their *Companions* for further pre-teaching.

PRE-TEACH Using the *Companions*

Reinforce the general idea. Use the selection and visual summaries presented on the first page of every selection in the *Companions*. These summaries will give students a framework to follow for understanding the selection. Use these tools to build familiarity, but do not use them as a replacement for reading.

Present audio summaries. The *Spanish/English Summaries Audio CD* can reinforce the main idea of a selection and provide extra support for students whose first language is Spanish.

Reinforce skills instruction. With your special education and special needs students and your English learners, use the Prepare to Read page in the *Reader's Companion Adapted Version* and the *Reader's Companion English Learner's Version* to reinforce Literary Analysis and Reading Strategy concepts. Written in simpler language and in basic sentence structures, the instruction will help students better grasp these ideas.

Provide decoding practice. Because many struggling readers, special education students, and English learners lack strategies for decoding bigger words, give them guided practice with the vocabulary words for the selection. Using the list, model a strategy for decoding polysyllabic words. First, show students how to break the word into parts and then put the parts back together to make a word.

> For the words *mimic* and *frightening,* ask students to draw a loop under each word part as they pronounce it.
>
> *mim ic*   *fright en ing*

Using this strategy, you can encourage students to look for familiar word parts and then break the rest of the word down into its consonant and vowel sounds. By building this routine regularly into your pre-teaching instruction, you reinforce a key reading skill for your students.

Prepare for lesson structure. To build students' ability to complete class-room activities, examine your lesson to see what types of language functions students will need to participate in. Look at these examples:

> If students are being asked to make predictions about upcoming paragraph content in an essay, review the power of transition words that act as signals to meaning. Rather than teaching all transitions, limit your instruction to the ones in the passages. Identify the key transition words and point out their meaning. In addition, teach students some basic sentence patterns and verbs to express opinions. Model for students statement patterns such as the following:
>
> *I predict that . . .*
>
> *Based on this transition word, I conclude that . . .*

TEACH Using the *Companions*

As average achieving students in your class read the selection in the textbook, allow your struggling readers to benefit from the extra guidance provided in *Reader's Companion.* Have your special education and special needs students and English learner's read the adapted version in the *Reader's Companion Adapted Version* or the *Reader's Companion English Learner's Version.* Whenever possible, give these students individualized attention by pairing them with aides, parent volunteers, or student peers.

Set purposes and limits. To keep students focused and motivated and to prevent them from becoming overwhelmed as they read a selection, clearly establish a reading purpose for students before assigning a manageable amount of text. Once you identify a focus question or a purpose, revisit the question occasionally as students read. You can do this with a brief whole-group dialogue or by encouraging students in pairs to remember the question. In addition, your effective modeling will also provide the scaffolding for students to begin internalizing these strategies for effective reading.

Model your thinking. Describe and model strategies for navigating different kinds of text. Use the questions raised in the side notes as a starting point. Then, explain how you arrive at an answer. Alternatively, ask a student to explain his or her responses to classmates.

Reinforce new vocabulary. Present key words when they occur within the context of the reading selection. Review the definition as it appears on the page. Then, make the words as concrete as possible by linking each to an object, a photo, or an idea.

Build interactivity. The side notes in the *Companions* are an excellent way to encourage student interactivity with the selections. To build students' ability to use these notes, model several examples with each selection. These are not busy work; they are activities that build fluency and provide the scaffolding necessary for student success.

Whenever possible, get students physically involved with the page, using *Mark the Text* icons as an invitation to use highlighters or colored pencils to circle, underline, or number key information. In addition, some students may find that using a small piece of cardboard or heavy construction paper helps to focus and guide their reading from one paragraph or page to the next.

Vary modes of instruction. To maintain student attention and interest, monitor and alternate the mode of instruction or activity. For example, alternate between teacher-facilitated and student-dominated reading activities. Assign brief amounts of text at a time, and alternate between oral, paired, and silent reading.

Monitor students' comprehension. As students use the side notes in the margins of the *Companions,* build-in opportunities to ensure that students are on purpose and understanding. Consider structured brief conversations for students to share, compare, or explain their thinking. Then, use these conversations to praise the correct use of strategies or to redirect students who need further support. In addition, this is an excellent chance for you to demonstrate your note-taking process and provide models of effective study notes for students to emulate.

Reinforce the reading experience. When students read the selection for the first time, they may be working on the decoding level. If time allows, students should read the selection twice to achieve a greater fluency and comfort level.

REVIEW AND ASSESS: Post-reading Activities

Reinforce writing and reading skills. Have students using the *Reader's Companion* complete the Reader's Response and Thinking About the Skill questions following the selection. Depending on the students' individual capabilities, you may assign them appropriate end-of-selection activities in the grade-level text.

Have students using the *Reader's Companion Adapted Version* and *Reader's Companion English Learner's Version* complete the Review and Assess page following the selection, and then assign the writing activity. Based on a writing activity presented in the grade-level text, the version in the *Adapted Reader's Version* and *English Learner's Version* provides guided, step-by-step support for students. By giving students the opportunities to show their reading comprehension and writing skills, you maintain reasonable expectations for their developing academic competence.

Model expectations. Make sure that students understand your assessment criteria in advance. Provide models of student work, whenever possible, for them to emulate, along with a non-model that fails to meet the specified assessment criteria. Do not provide exemplars that are clearly outside of their developmental range. Save student work that can later serve as a model for students with different levels of academic preparation.

Lead students to closure. To achieve closure, ask students to end the class session by writing three to five outcome statements about their experience in the day's lesson, expressing both new understandings and needs for clarification.

Encourage self-monitoring and self-assessment. Remember to provide safe opportunities for students to alert you to any learning challenges they are experiencing. Consider having students submit anonymous written questions (formulated either independently or with a partner) about confusing lesson content. Later, you can follow up on these points of confusion at the end of class or in the subsequent class session.

EXTEND Using the Student Edition

Present the unabridged selection for students who read the adapted version. Build in opportunities for students to read the full selection in the grade-level textbook. This will allow them to apply familiar concepts and vocabulary and stretch their literacy muscles.

Play an audio reading of the unabridged selection. Use the *Listening to Literature Audiotapes* or *CDs*. Students who read the adapted version may benefit from reading along while listening to a professional recording of the selection. Encourage students to use their fingertips to follow the words as they are read.

Invite reader response. When students have finished reviewing the selection—whether in a *Companion* or in the grade-level textbook—include all students in your class in post-reading analysis. To guide an initial discussion, use the Respond question in the *Thinking About the Selection* section in the textbook. You will find that questions such as the following examples will provide strong springboards for classroom interaction:

> **Respond:** What advice would you have given the mother and daughter? Why?

Respond: What questions would you like to ask the writer about his experience?

Respond: Do you find the boy's actions courageous, touching, or silly? Why or why not?

Encourage students to explain their answers to these questions by supporting their ideas with evidence from the text or their own lives. In addition, invite students to respond to classmates' ideas. These questions will lead students from simply getting the gist of a selection to establishing a personal connection to the lesson content.

Direct student analysis with scaffolded questions. When you are ready to move students into the Review and Assess questions, let your average achieving students use the instruction and questions in the grade-level textbook. At the same time, encourage special education and special needs students and English learners to use the questions in the *Reader's Companion Adapted Version* and the *Reader's Companion English Learner's Version.*

- Questions in the *Companions*, written in more simple language and providing more explicit support, will be more accessible to these students. Students will be applying concepts and practicing strategies at their own level.

- Some special education or special needs students or English learners may be prepared to answer questions in the grade-level text. The two-part questions in the *Thinking About the Selection* section are written to build and support student analysis. First, students use lower-level thinking skills to identify information or to recall important details in a selection. For the second part, students use a higher-level thinking skill based on the answer to the first part.

Look at these examples of scaffolded questions from the grade-level textbook:

(a) Recall: Why does the boy tell his father to leave the sickroom?
(b) Infer: What does this reveal about the boy?

(a) Recall: Why does the boy think he will die?
(b) Infer: What is the meaning of the title?

Revisit and reinforce strategies. Recycle pre- and post-reading tasks regularly so that students can become more familiar with the task process and improve their performance. If they are constantly facing curricular novelty, special education and special needs students never have the opportunity to refine their skills and demonstrate improved competence. For example, if you ask them to identify a personality trait of an essential character in a story and then support this observation with relevant details in an expository paragraph, it would make sense to have them write a similar paragraph in the near future about another character.

Show students how to transfer skills. Consider ways in which students can transfer knowledge and skills gleaned from one assignment/lesson to a subsequent lesson. For example, discuss with students the ways in which they can apply new vocabulary and language strategies outside of the classroom. In addition, demonstrate the applicability of new reading and writing strategies to real-world literacy tasks. Include periodic writing tasks for an authentic audience other than the teacher, such as another class, fellow classmates, local businesses, family, etc.

Offer praise and encourage growth. Praise students' efforts to experiment with new language in class, both in writing and in speaking.

Teaching Part 2: Reading Informational Materials

Part 2 of the *Reader's Companion*, the *Reader's Companion Adapted Version*, and the *Reader's Companion English Learner's Version* presents unabridged versions of all of the Reading Informational Materials features from the student book. As in Part 1, questions prompt students to interact with the text in a variety of ways, helping them gain competence in reading informational materials such as newspaper articles, business documents, and product directions and warranties.

The prereading page for each selection previews the type of informational material in the lesson and presents the reading strategy that is addressed in the student edition. The **Build Understanding** box introduces vocabulary and specialized terms that are specific to the selection.

The selection pages include many of the same types of side notes that appear in Part 1. Additional **Reading Informational Materials** notes focus on specific features of informational materials.

In the *Reader's Companion Adapted Version* and the *Reader's Companion English Learner's Version*, a **Review and Assess** page follows each selection. This page provides additional support for special needs students and English learner's by focusing on reading comprehension, reading strategies, and brief writing activities.

Helping Students Use the Vocabulary Builder Pages

The **Vocabulary Builder** appears at the end of each *Companion*. These pages provide a place for students to record new vocabulary words that they encounter in the selections. Remind students to use these pages and to continue the Vocabulary Builder in their notebooks if they run out of room. Periodically, you may want to allow volunteers to share original sentences that contain the vocabulary words they have chosen.

Answers to Part 1
Unit 1

"The Cat Who Thought She Was A Dog and The Dog Who Thought He Was A Cat" by Isaac Bashevis Singer

p. 5 Activate Prior Knowledge: Students may say that people might be shocked by their looks or might spend a lot of time staring at themselves.

p. 5 Reading Strategy: 1. The animals are imitating each other. 2. Mimic means to copy or imitate.

p. 5 Reading Check: They are most interested in the mirror.

p. 6 Reading Strategy: Students should underline "first payment" and "get his money back."

p. 6 Reading Strategy: They didn't do the rest of the chores.

p. 7 Reading Strategy: Students should circle "saw her image in the mirror," and the second sentence.

p. 7 Stop to Reflect: Students should say that the Skibas were happy with the way they looked.

p. 7 Literary Analysis: Students should underline the section in quotation marks in the last paragraph beginning, "A glass mirror shows only . . ." They should restate the moral in their own words.

p. 7 Reader's Response: Students may say that they wouldn't worry about how they looked. They may also say they would spend less time deciding what to wear.

"Two Kinds" by Amy Tan

p. 9 Activate Prior Knowledge: Answers will vary, but students should explain why they believe whether it is or is not possible to expect too much from another person.

p. 9 Literary Analysis: Students should circle, "her mother and father, her family home, her first husband, and two daughters, twin baby girls."

p. 9 Reading Check: Her mother wants her to be like Shirley Temple.

p. 10 Reading Strategy: Students should circle "patient." Their definition should read "not able to wait calmly."

p. 10 Reading Strategy: Students should say that they find the word sort and the suffix -ment.

p. 10 Reading Check: She feels excited about becoming a prodigy at first.

p. 11 Reading Strategy: Students should circle "expect."

p. 11 Literary Analysis: She is reacting to her own anger about her mother's expectations and demands.

p. 11 Reading Check: She decides to stop trying.

p. 12 Reading Check: She is fascinated by the performance.

p. 12 Literary Analysis: She may do it just because she wants to disagree with her mother.

p. 12 Literary Analysis: 1. The mother gets a piano and piano lessons for her daughter. 2. Her motive is wanting her daughter to be very good at something.

p. 13 Reading Strategy: Students should circle "grateful" and define ungrateful as "not grateful" or "not thankful" or "not appreciative."

p. 13 Reading Strategy: The word is "reach."

p. 13 Reading Check: She learns that Old Chong does not see well enough to tell when she is playing wrong notes.

p. 14 Literary Analysis: She does not want to do what her mother wants her to do.

p. 14 Literary Analysis: She wants to boast about her daughter.

p. 15 Reading Check: Students should circle "Schumann."

p. 15 Reading Strategy: Students should circle "nervous" and underline *-ness*.

p. 15 Reading Strategy: Students should define envisioned as "imagined."

p. 15 Reading Check: She starts making mistakes.

p. 16 Literary Analysis: He thinks she has played wonderfully.

p. 16 Reading Strategy: Students should circle "honor." Since an honor is like a reward, honorable mention must also be something positive. Also, the words "first prize" are a clue to its meaning.

p. 16 Reading Check: Her mother's response hurts the most.

p. 17 Literary Analysis: Students should circle "angry."

p. 17 Reading Strategy: fright or frighten; My mother was so strong she frightened me.

p. 17 Reading Check: She tries to force her daughter to play again.

p. 18 Reading Strategy: Students should circle "speak" and underline *un-* and *-able*. Unspeakable means "cannot be spoken about."

p. 18 Reading Check: Her mother offers her the piano.

p. 19 Stop to Reflect: She seems to have made peace with her mother. She is no longer angry, but instead is caring for her mother's things in a way that shows she cherishes her memory.

p. 19 Literary Analysis: The clues it gives are in talking about the two different piano pieces. The author may have wanted to show that she has learned that there are two sides to her, not just one.

p. 19 Reader's Response: Responses will vary but should have advice based on information from the story.

p. 19 Thinking About the Skill: Students may say that they learned to take words apart to find a word they recognized.

"My Furthest-Back Person" by Alex Haley

p. 21 Activate Prior Knowledge: Possible response: Where did my family come from?

p. 21 Literary Analysis: Students should underline I wherever it appears, and "across the interim years I had thought of Grandma's stories" and "I wouldn't have dreamed of admitting . . . forbears."

p. 21 Reading Strategy: "I looked upon the names of Grandma's parents. . . ."

p. 21 Reading Check: He found the names of his great-grandparents and great aunts and uncles.

p. 22 Reading Strategy: Students should circle "I" and write Alex Haley. Students should circle "I was awed."

p. 22 Reading Check: Haley wants to find out what language his ancestors spoke.

p. 22 Stop to Reflect: If he learns what language they spoke, it will help him pinpoint where they came from.

p. 23 Stop to Reflect: He understands from Dr. Vansina that that is where his family probably came from and he wants to go there to learn more.

p. 23 Reading Strategy: Students should circle "in places in the back country lived very old men . . . who could tell centuries of the histories of certain very old family clans."

p. 23: Reading Check: Dr. Vansina recognized the sounds of the language Haley knew as Mandinka, and thought that some of the words were those meaning Gambia River.

p. 24 Reading Check: He thinks he will be able to learn about his family from the griot.

p. 24 Reading Strategy: It describes the man: he was small, wearing a pill-box hat and white robe.

p. 24 Reading Check: It is a well built to provide water for traveling groups of enslaved Africans.

p. 25 Literary Analysis: They show that the person speaking kept pausing to listen to the griot.

p. 25 Stop to Reflect: Possible response: He knew that the griot was talking about his ancestors who'd gone to the United States. It affected him strongly.

p. 25 Reading Check: He symbolizes all of the people who were taken away from them.

p. 26 Reading Check: He gets them when the history the griot is telling agrees with the history he knows from his grandmother. He knows that he is hearing his own family's history.

p. 26 Literary Analysis: He bursts into tears.

p. 27 Reading Check: He is searching for the name of the ship that brought his ancestor to Annapolis. He finds a reference to British soldiers being sent to the Gambia region. This identifies the correct time-the griot had mentioned soldiers.

p. 27 Stop to Reflect: Possible response: 1. Haley is very curious about his family's past. 2. He is an excellent researcher. 3. He is an emotional person who feels things deeply.

p. 27 Reader's Response: Possible questions: What discovery was the most exciting for you? How did your family react when you told your news?

p. 27 Thinking About the Skill: First, find the subject of the sentence. Then find out what the sentence tells about the subject.

"A Day's Wait"
by Ernest Hemingway

p. 29 Activate Prior Knowledge: Students may describe being bored, lonely, or in discomfort.

p. 29 Reading Strategy: Miserable means "in a bad state."

p. 29 Reading Check: He has a headache and a fever.

p. 30 Reading Strategy: They have something to do with writing.

p. 30 Literary Analysis: Students should circle "boy had refused . . . ," "You can't come in," and "Staring still . . ."

p. 31 Literary Analysis: He believes that he is going to die soon.

p. 31 Reading Strategy: A kilometer is one thousand meters or approximately three thousand feet.

p. 31 Reader's Response: Possible responses: I think the boy was brave because he was trying not to show how scared he was about dying. I think the boy was foolish because if he had just told what was going on, his father would have explained that he was not dying.

p. 31 Thinking About the Skill: When you recognize a root in an unfamiliar word, you know the meaning of the word's root as well.

"Was Tarzan a Three-Bandage Man?"
by Bill Cosby

p. 33 Activate Prior Knowledge: Students should describe an instance of imitating someone or give a description of someone they admire.

p. 33 Reading Strategy: Emulate means "imitate" or "copy."

p. 33 Reading Check: He imitates them.

p. 34 Literary Analysis: Cosby's mother admires educated people; Cosby admires athletes. His mother values education; he values strength and athleticism.

p. 34 Reading Strategy: Attire is something you wear.

p. 34 Reader's Response: Students should take a position on imitating or not imitating sports heroes and explain why they chose as they did.

p. 34 Thinking About the Skill: Students may say that they find clues in surrounding words and phrases that give them more information about an unfamiliar word.

Unit 2

"*from* In Search of Our Mothers' Gardens" by Alice Walker

p. 36 Activate Prior Knowledge: Students should describe a person they find inspiring and give two or three reasons for their admiration.

p. 36 Literary Analysis: Students' answers should include three of the following: 1) She made all their clothing; 2) she made all their towels and sheets; 3) she canned vegetables and fruit; 4) she made quilts; 5) she labored in the fields; 6) her day began before sunup and continued until late at night.

p. 36 Stop to Reflect: Students' answers should reflect the quilt's uniqueness, beauty, age, and historical value.

p. 37 Reading Strategy: The name of the maker of the quilt is not known (that is, the quilt is "without name" attached to it).

p. 37 Literary Analysis: Students should underline at least two of these ideas: 1) "no song or poem will bear my mother's name" 2) "so many of the stories that I write . . . are my mother's stories" 3) "through years of listening to my mother's stories of her life, I have absorbed not only the stories themselves, but something of the manner in which she spoke."

p. 37 Reading Check: Students should underline the sentence "For stories, too, were subject to being distracted, to dying without conclusion."

p. 38 Reading Strategy: *Spirea: Speiraia* means "spire"; its definition is "shrubs of the rose family with dense clusters of small pink or white flowers."

p. 38 Literary Analysis: Students should underline the sentences, "I hear again the praise showered on her because whatever rocky soil she landed on, she turned into a garden" and ". . . to this day people drive by our house in Georgia—perfect strangers and imperfect strangers—and ask to stand or walk among my mother's art."

p. 38 Reading Check: The poem is about the women of Walker's generation. It is written by Walker.

p. 39 Reading Check: The mission of "the generals" is to discover books and desks and to find a place for their children.

p. 39 Literary Analysis: Walker pays tribute to her—and her black sisters'—foremothers.

p. 39 Reading Strategy: *Bio-* means "life."

p. 39 Reader's Response: Students' answers should mention one skill in the family, such as singing, and discuss how that skill might have been passed down. They should also speculate how that person or their family might be different without that skill.

"Seventh Grade" by Gary Soto

p. 41 Activate Prior Knowledge: Students should describe their concerns and feelings about the first day of seventh grade.

p. 41 Reading Strategy: 1. The idiom is "making a face." 2. Its word-for-word meaning is "creating a face." 3. Its idiomatic meaning is "distorting the face, especially the mouth and eyes, on purpose to achieve a desired effect."

p. 41 Reading Check: He decides to study French because he would like to visit France, and also because a girl he likes is taking it.

p. 42 Literary Analysis: Students should circle two of the following: 'bout, ain't so good, that's for sure, socked each other, that's weird, making a face.

p. 42 Reading Check: He thinks the scowling is strange. However, when he tries it, a girl looks at him, so he thinks it must work.

p. 42 Reading Strategy: The idiom is "to catch her eye." Victor tries to get her attention.

p. 43 Literary Analysis: Students could underline any third person pronoun (he/she); the sentence "So much for being in the same class, he thought." (shows a character's thoughts); and the sentence "They knew he had a crush on Teresa." (shows the thoughts of several characters)

p. 43 Stop to Reflect: Because idioms are used in casual speech or writing, they make the tone informal, light, and casual.

p. 43 Reading Check: He thinks people will make fun of him if his interest in Teresa shows, and he doesn't want Teresa to know he likes her until he can see how she feels.

p. 44 Literary Analysis: Students should underline "One kid," "What's," or "bluff his way out."

p. 44 Reading Check: Students should underline "La me vave me con le grandma." It doesn't mean anything. It's a mishmash of French, Spanish, and English words.

p. 44 Reading Check: He is trying to impress Teresa.

p. 45 Literary Analysis: The reader knows Mr. Bueller is reminiscing about his own youth.

p. 45 Reading Check: He empathizes with Victor because he remembers a similar experience he had trying to impress a girl while he was in college. Therefore, he plays along with Victor's pretense of speaking French.

p. 45 Stop to Reflect: Victor is going to like seventh grade because Teresa does not discover that he is faking his knowledge of French and because she is friendly and wants to study with him.

p. 45 Reader's Response: Students' responses should show some understanding of motives like Victor's attempt to impress a girl.

p. 45 Thinking About the Skill: You would only know Victor's thoughts and not those of the other characters. You would see everything through Victor's eyes.

"Melting Pot" by Anna Quindlen

p. 47 Activate Prior Knowledge: Students should describe a typical city neighborhood, including such things as rows of apartment buildings, corner grocery store, people sitting on the stoop, children playing street hockey or jump rope, people of different ethnic backgrounds, etc.

p. 47 Literary Analysis: Students should circle such words as "weekly tabloid," "on a macro level," "new moneyed professionals," "suspicious," "bigots," "on a micro level."

p. 47 Reading Check: 1) The newspaper makes it sound as if everybody hates everybody else. 2) In reality, they all get along pretty well as individuals.

p. 48 Reading Check: Students should underline the sentence "A lot of old Italians lived around me, which suited me just fine because I was the granddaughter of old Italians."

p. 48 Literary Analysis: 1. You know the thoughts of one person, Quindlen. 2. Yes, Quindlen uses the pronoun *I* to refer to herself. 3. Yes, the narrator takes part in the events she describes. 4. The story is told in the first person.

p. 48 Reading Strategy: "The baby slips out with the bath water." The idiom means that good things sometimes leave or are thrown out with the bad.

p. 49 Reading Check: Because of the many types of people from different ethnic and economic backgrounds, there is an "us vs. them" feeling in the neighborhood that could "boil over" into more than just silent resentment.

p. 49 Stop to Reflect: Good things: People from many backgrounds; people get along one-on-one; it is a vibrant, lively place; people are concerned about similar things, like conditions of the streets. Bad things: many people have negative, prejudiced attitudes about people not like themselves; there is a "us vs. them" mentality.

p. 49 Reader's Response: Students should give reasons why they might like or dislike the neighborhood.

p. 49 Thinking About the Skill: Look at the author's choice of words. If the author uses slang and idiomatic and everyday speech, the tone is not formal. If the author uses formal, educated words, it is formal. The subject matter helps determine the tone.

"The Hummingbird That Lived Through Winter" by William Saroyan

p. 51 Activate Prior Knowledge: Students' answers should describe caring for a sick or hurt animal.

p. 51 Reading Check: Students should underline "Plants, bushes, trees—all strong, . . ."

p. 51 Reading Strategy: You find the word *guard*. Knowing the meaning of a word part or a smaller word within a larger word allow you to make a better guess at the word's meaning.

p. 52 Reading Strategy: Students should circle *form* in the word *transformation*. 1. It is a word root. 2. *Form* means "shape." 3. The word means *change form*.

p. 52 Reading Strategy: Students should circle *ap-* and underline *pear-* in *appeared;* circle *-less* and underline *rest-* in *restless;* circle *de-* and underline *scrib-* in *describing*.

p. 52 Reading Check: He lets it go free because it has regained its spirits and is now restless and wants to go.

p. 53 Literary Analysis: Students' answers should indicate that the hummingbird represents all life.

p. 53 Stop to Reflect: Dikran means that we humans have the responsibility of being the caretakers of all life.

p. 53 Reader's Response: Some students may say that they would have kept the bird inside to protect it, others may say that they would have released it because it seemed to want to go.

p. 53 Thinking About the Skill: Students' responses should contain some of the following ideas: Symbols make it easier for readers to relate to what the writer is saying because symbols usually have the same or a similar meaning for most people. Symbols also evoke an emotional response. The use of symbols makes the language vivid and often beautiful.

Unit 3

"The Third Wish" by Joan Aiken

p. 55 Activate Prior Knowledge: Students should answer with a wish of their own.

p. 55 Reading Strategy: Students should circle "struggling" and "as if somebody was in trouble."

p. 55 Reading Check: The swan swims into the river, preening, then turns into a small man in dressed in green and wearing a gold crown.

p. 56 Literary Analysis: Students should circle "threateningly."

p. 56 Reading Check: The leaves represent three wishes.

p. 56 Stop to Reflect: Possible response: He did make a wise choice. He was lonely, and his wife will keep him company.

p. 57 Reading Strategy: Students should circle "wandered much in the garden" and "she would return . . . with no explanation."

p. 57 Literary Analysis: Mr. Peters has a car and a briefcase.

p. 57 Reading Check: He sees her with a swan and she tells him the swan is her sister.

p. 58 Literary Analysis: He is a kind man who puts his wife's happiness above his own.

p. 58 Stop to Reflect: Possible response: I like both Mr. Peters and Leita very much. Mr. Peters is kind in wanting Leita to be happy. Leita does not want to abandon Mr. Peters. Their situation makes me sad, because it seems like they can't both be happy at the same time.

p. 58 Reading Check: Students should underline the sentence beginning, "He stooped down and kissed her goodbye . . ." He wishes for Leita to be turned back into a swan.

p. 59 Stop to Reflect: Possible response: I think he used his wish well. I was not surprised, because he had already offered to turn Leita back into a swan.

p. 59 Reading Strategy: Students should circle "when thieves tried to break into his house" and "carried them off bodily and dropped them in the river." Set upon means "attacked."

p. 59 Reader's Response: Students may say that they would have wished for things rather than for a person.

p. 59 Thinking About the Skill: Students may say that nearby words restate the unfamiliar word or give examples of it.

"The Charge of the Light Brigade" by Alfred, Lord Tennyson

p. 61 Activate Prior Knowledge: Students should describe two images of war.

p. 61 Literary Analysis: Students should circle "Theirs not to" in lines 13 and 14, and "Theirs" and "to" in line 15. "Theirs" refers to the soldiers.

p. 61 Reading Check: The Light Brigade was a group of 600 soldiers entering into a battle.

p. 62 Reading Strategy: Students should circle "gun."

p. 62 Literary Analysis: Students may say that repeating the word makes it seem like the soldiers are surrounded by canons.

p. 62 Reading Check: The poet is proud of the soldiers. He says they fought well, that we should honor their charge, and asks when their glory will fade.

p. 62 Reader's Response: Students may say that they feel as thought they have been through a battle.

"The Californian's Tale" by Mark Twain

p. 64 Activate Prior Knowledge: Possible response: My grandparents live in a small white house with beautiful flowers and a well-groomed lawn. Inside everything is very neat and clean. I can tell my grandparents are proud of their house and want things to look cared-for.

p. 64 Literary Analysis: Students should underline "busy little city with banks and newspapers and fire companies and a

mayor and aldermen had been," and "prettiest little cottage homes, snug and cozy."

p. 64 Reading Check: He prospects for gold.

p. 65 Reading Strategy: It has many flowers outside, and inside there are furnishings like a rug, prints, books and other small touches that make it feel like a home.

p. 65 Reading Check: It has lots of homey touches that make it very comfortable.

p. 66 Stop to Reflect: Students may say they like the pride the man takes in his home and the woman who did the work.

p. 66 Literary Analysis: Students should circle all details in the first sentence, beginning with "white counterpane."

p. 66 Reading Check: He hopes the visitor will notice something in the room.

p. 67 Stop to Reflect: He seems to worship her: he admires all she's done in the house, and is eager for the visitor to admire her, too.

p. 67 Reading Check: The narrator wants to meet the wife of the cottage owner.

p. 67 Reading Strategy: The narrator decides to stay to meet the wife. The two men stay up late talking, spend the next day together, and receive a visitor at twilight.

p. 68 Stop to Reflect: Students may think Tom's response is a little odd. It seems excessive for him to cry on hearing a letter from his friend's wife when it doesn't contain bad news.

p. 68 Reading Check: Students should circle "I was taking out my watch pretty often."

p. 69 Reading Strategy: They are waiting for the wife to arrive. The narrator feels impatient with Henry for being so worried and speaks harshly to him. Henry takes it badly, and the narrator is ashamed. Charley arrives and works to improve the situation and make Henry feel better.

p. 69 Literary Analysis: Students should circle "make your mind easy," "don't you fret," and "as sure as you are born."

p. 69 Reading Check: Joe tells him to take the other glass.

p. 70 Reading Strategy: She was married to Henry at age nineteen. Six months after their marriage, she was captured by Indians on her way back from visiting her family.

p. 70 Reading Check: She was captured by Indians nineteen years ago and hasn't been seen since.

p. 70 Reader's Response: Students may say that they were surprised by the ending because Henry gives no sign that she is not still living, or they may say that they suspected something was wrong from Tom's response to the letter or Joe's stopping the narrator from taking a particular glass.

p. 70 Thinking About the Skill: Students may report that they were better able to keep track of the plot by summarizing.

"Four Skinny Trees" by Sandra Cisneros

p. 72 Activate Prior Knowledge: Students should tell about a special place and how it makes them feel.

p. 72 Reading Strategy: Students should circle "tulips" or "tulips in a glass."

p. 72 Literary Analysis: On a deeper level the trees stand for the writer's personal growth.

p. 72 Reading Check: Their secret is their strength.

p. 72 Reader's Response: Students may or may not feel as the author does, but should explain the strength of their connection to trees.

p. 72 Thinking About the Skill: Students may say that figurative language adds depth and variety to language.

Unit 4

"The Night the Bed Fell" by James Thurber

p. 74 Activate Prior Knowledge: Students should relate a humorous event that wouldn't have seemed funny when it happened.

p. 74 Reading Check: Students should underline the sentence "It happened, then, that my father had decided to sleep in the attic one night, to be away where he could think."

p. 74 Reading Strategy: It mentions that the bed fell one night.

p. 75 Reading Strategy: They do not move the story forward, so they are not significant events.

p. 75 Reading Check: Students should circle "Old Aunt Melissa Beall," "Aunt Sarah Shoaf," and "Aunt Gracie Shoaf," and underline "destined to die on South High Street"; either "blow chloroform under her door" or "she always piled her money . . ."; and one of the passages about throwing shoes.

p. 75 Literary Analysis: Each relative has an odd belief. Most of them behave strangely as a result. Their strange behavior is funny.

p. 76 Reading Strategy: It must be significant because the title of the story refers to a bed falling.

p. 76 Literary Analysis: Everything he does is exaggerated, which makes it funny.

p. 76 Reading Check: Students should underline "her worst dread was realized: the big wooden bed upstairs had fallen on father"; "He thought, that mother had become, for no apparent reason, hysterical"; and "Briggs . . . came to the quick conclusion that he was suffocating."

p. 77 Literary Analysis: Students should underline some of the following:
1) "Get me out of this!" I bawled
2) "Gugh," gasped Briggs . . .
3) . . . mother, still shouting . . .
4) Her frantic pulls only added to the general banging . . . 5) Roy and the dog were now up, the one shouting questions, the other barking.6) "I'm coming, I'm coming!" he wailed . . .

p. 77 Reading Check: Thurber's mother and brother Herman are trying to get into the attic, Roy and Rex are there, yelling and barking, Briggs and Thurber join them and the dog attacks Briggs. Roy gets Rex and holds him. Roy jerks the door open.

p. 77 Stop to Reflect: Students may suggest that the father first made it clear that nothing had happened to him. Then, if someone asked about the loud crash, Thurber might have explained that his bed had tipped over, and one by one, people would have explained what they knew as well as what they thought had actually happened.

p. 77 Reader's Response: Possible response: I thought the scene in which Briggs dumped camphor on himself was the funniest.

p. 77 Thinking About the Skill: Students may say that they would be able to follow the plot of a story or novel more easily by identifying the events that matter most.

"All Summer in A Day" by Ray Bradbury

p. 79 Activate Prior Knowledge: Students should describe an experience of being excluded or of excluding someone else.

p. 79 Literary Analysis: Students should circle "planet Venus" and underline two of the following: "It had been raining for seven years. . . ."; ". . . with the sweet crystal fall of showers and the concussion of storms so heavy they were tidal waves . . ."; "A thousand forests had been crushed under the rain. . . ."

p. 79 Reading Check: The children hope the sun will come out.

p. 80 Reading Strategy: 1. He is rude to Margot, asking her what she's looking at, demanding that she answer him. He pushes her. 2. She doesn't say anything and doesn't move on her own. 3. They are very different.

p. 80 Reading Strategy: Students should underline ". . . she would play no games with them in the echoing tunnels of the underground city" and "When the class sang songs about happiness and life and games her lips barely moved."

p. 80 Literary Analysis: Students should underline the sentence, "And then, of course, the biggest crime of all was that she had come here only five years ago from Earth, and she remembered the sun and the way the sun was and the sky was when she was four in Ohio."

p. 81 Stop to Reflect: A shower reminds her too much of the constant rain, and she can't stand the wetness anymore.

p. 81 Literary Analysis: If they lived in a place where the sun came out regularly, Margot might not have been so sad, and she would not have been so different from the other children.

p. 81 Reading Check: She is waiting for the sun to come out.

p. 81 Reading Check: Students should underline the sentence beginning "They surged about her. . . ."

p. 82 Stop to Reflect: Students may say they would be very excited and happy to see the sun.

p. 82 Reading Check: This is only the second time in their lives that they have seen the sun and they don't really remember the first time, since they were very young.

p. 82 Literary Analysis: The description on the first page was mainly about water-storms and tidal waves crushing the forests. This description is about how blue the sky is and how the jungle burns with sunlight.

p. 83 Reading Check: Students should underline three of the following:
1) The children lay out, laughing, on the jungle mattress . . . 2) They ran among the trees . . . 3) . . . they played hide-and-seek and tag . . . 4) . . . they squinted at the sun until tears ran down their faces . . . 5) . . . they put their hands up to the yellowness . . . 6) . . . they breathed of the fresh, fresh air . . . 7) . . . listened to the silence . . . 8) They looked at everything and savored everything. 9) . . . they ran and ran in shouting circles.

p. 83 Literary Analysis: Students may respond that Margot's classmates will understand Margot better and will be kinder to her now that they have seen the sun and lost it again.

p. 83 Reading Check: Students should circle "Then one of them gave a little cry."

p. 84 Stop to Reflect: She is probably feeling more hopeless than ever.

p. 84 Reading Strategy: Margot is feeling sad and hopeless. The other children are feeling guilty and probably upset.

p. 84 Reader's Response: Students may feel compassion for Margot and how she is treated.

p. 84 Thinking About the Skill: Students may report that contrasting the characters made the conflict clearer because it pointed out the differences between the children.

"The Highwayman" by Alfred Noyes

p. 86 Activate Prior Knowledge: Students should write about a time they did something difficult in order to help someone.

p. 86 Reading Check: Students should underline three of the following:
1) He'd a French cocked-hat on his forehead . . . 2) . . . a bunch of lace at his chin . . . 3) A coat of claret velvet . . . 4) . . . breeches of brown doe skin . . . 5) His boots were up to the thigh. 6) His pistol butts a-twinkle . . . 7) His rapier hilt a-twinkle . . .

p. 86 Reading Check: Bess, the landlord's daughter, is waiting for him.

p. 87 Literary Analysis: Students should underline the phrase, "His eyes were hollows of madness . . ."

p. 87 Reading Strategy: Students may say that the landlord's daughter or the highwayman will get in trouble.

p. 87 Literary Analysis: The repetition of the phrase "by moonlight" adds to the suspense by its sound and the intense feeling it gives. Also, the last line suggests that seeing Bess could be difficult and that something bad might happen to the highwayman.

p. 88 Reading Strategy: Tim must have reported what he heard to the soldiers.

p. 88 Literary Analysis: Students should circle the word "doomed."

p. 88 Reading Check: The soldiers are using the woman as bait to capture the highwayman.

p. 89 Literary Analysis: The reader is left waiting to find out whether or not she will pull the trigger.

p. 89 Stop to Reflect: Students may say that she wants to fire the gun as a warning.

p. 89 Reading Check: She shoots herself to warn the highwayman that there is danger for him at the inn.

p. 89 Reading Check: The highwayman turns his horse around and flees.

p. 90 Reading Strategy: Students should underline "and died in the darkness there."

p. 90 Reading Check: The soldiers shoot him as he rides.

p. 90 Stop to Reflect: Students may note that they are written in italic type, that the suspense of the poem is over now, or that they are written about a later time when people claim to see the ghosts of Bess and the highwayman.

p. 90 Reader's Response: Students may say that Bess is braver, since she was willing to kill herself to warn the highwayman.

p. 90 Thinking About the Skill: One event causes another. The first event is the cause, the second is the effect.

"Amigo Brothers" by Piri Thomas

p. 92 Activate Prior Knowledge: Students may say that someone preparing for a fight would want to do weight training, aerobic exercise, and get plenty of practice in the ring.

p. 92 Reading Strategy: Students should infer that neither boy comes from a wealthy family.

p. 92 Literary Analysis: This story is told from the third person point of view.

p. 93 Literary Analysis: 1) The narrator is outside of story (he uses third person "they"). 2) The narrator knows the boys' thoughts.

p. 93 Stop to Reflect: Students may say that they would have conflicting feelings of wanting to win but not wanting to beat or hurt a friend.

p. 93 Reading Check: They both dream of going far in boxing, and the winner of this fight will get to go to the Golden Gloves Tournament.

p. 94 Reading Strategy: Possible response: Felix and Antonio admire and respect each other. They do not want to hurt each other, but neither fighter wants to give up the chance to become a champion.

p. 94 Stop to Reflect: They think it would complicate things since they are preparing to meet as strangers in the ring.

p. 94 Reading Check: Students should underline the sentence beginning "After, the fight, we can get it together . . ."

p. 95 Reading Check: Students should underline the sentence beginning "It was Felix the Champion vs. . . ." and write the sentence "To spare Felix hurt, he would have to knock him out, early and quick."

p. 95 Reading Strategy: The boys probably see that he is a good fighter, and they don't want to get hurt.

p. 95 Literary Analysis: Neither of them knows that the other is hoping for a knock-out in the first round so as not to hurt the other. The effect on the audience is to be sympathetic to and like both boys.

p. 96 Reading Strategy: Students should circle the details about the posters advertising the fight and about the boys' popularity.

p. 96 Literary Analysis: Students should circle "hoping to avoid seeing Antonio."

p. 96 Reading Check: It was moved because the gym was too small for everyone who wanted to see the fight.

p. 97 Stop to Reflect: He is glad to stop thinking about the fight and finally get it underway.

p. 97 Reading Strategy: Students may infer that both boys are feeling somewhat nervous. Details circled may include "Antonio tried to be cool" and "both as one, . . . turned away to face his own corner."

p. 97 Literary Analysis: The third person lets the reader know that the announcer is pleased with being able to speak in two languages.

p. 97 Reading Check: The fight can't end in a tie because only one fighter can go on to compete in the Golden Gloves.

p. 98 Reading Strategy: You can infer that they are both good athletes and good sports.

p. 98 Stop to Reflect: The fight is going well for Tony. He got in some good punches and was not too badly hurt.

p. 98 Reading Check: Antonio moves well and has a long reach. Felix has a very hard punch.

p. 99 Literary Analysis: 1) The use of the pronoun he indicates that it is in third person. 2) The narrator knows Antonio's thoughts.

p. 99 Reading Strategy: They are both determined to win.

p. 99 Reading Check: Both have been hurt, but they are still able to fight.

p. 100 Reading Strategy: Students should circle the section beginning "Antonio came out fast," "Felix . . . commenced his attack anew," and the next paragraph, beginning "Both pounded away."

p. 100 Reading Check: Once the boys realize the fight is over, they rush towards each other and hug. Then, without waiting for the announcement of the winner, they leave the ring arm in arm.

p. 100 Reader's Response: Students may say that they were surprised that the boys left the ring without finding out who won since they had both been so determined to be the winner.

p. 100 Thinking About the Skill: Students may say that making inferences gave them added insight into why the characters behaved as they did.

"Our Finest Hour" by Charles Osgood

p. 102 Activate Prior Knowledge: Students should share one or two mistakes from something they have seen, read, or heard about.

p. 102 Reading Strategy: The author's purpose is probably to entertain.

p. 102 Reading Check: Students may say that all of the regular workers were missing, or they may say that the newscast has gone very badly.

p. 103 Literary Analysis: Students may underline "What came up was a series of pictures of people who seemed to be dead" and the sentence beginning "In the fishbowl, . . ."

p. 103 Reading Strategy: It is understated. With so many problems, this is probably the worst news broadcast ever seen.

p. 103 Reading Check: The worst part is when the sound of someone yelling inside the station gets transmitted to the audience.

p. 104 Stop to Reflect: His message might be that things go wrong when too many people don't know what they are doing. He gets it across very successfully by including many details about the newscast.

p. 104 Reader's Response: Students should retell the section they found most amusing.

p. 104 Thinking About the Skill: Students may say that they will read more carefully if they know an author is trying to persuade them about something.

"Cat on the Go" by James Herriot

p. 106 Activate Prior Knowledge: Students should relate a story about a lost pet.

p. 106 Reading Check: He is extremely thin, and his intestines are hanging out of his body.

p. 107 Literary Analysis: Students should underline "whistled under his breath," and "drew the tip of his forefinger again and again across the furry cheek." He shows that he cares about cats and feels badly about what has happened to this particular cat.

p. 107 Reading Check: He faces a decision about whether to end the cat's life or try to save it.

p. 108 Reading Strategy: He is referring to the exposed intestines.

p. 108 Literary Analysis: They don't give up easily. They want to preserve life.

p. 108 Reading Check: They perform surgery to try to save the cat's life.

p. 109 Literary Analysis: Students should underline all details relating to Helen's words and actions. Her words and actions tell you that she cares about cats and that she is a nurturing sort of person.

p. 109 Literary Analysis: When she gets the box to put the cat in, she demonstrates the first meaning, and when she sits and thinks, she demonstrates the second.

p. 109 Reading Check: Helen is talking to him.

p. 110 Stop to Reflect: Naming someone implies they are going to be around long enough to need a name.

p. 110 Reading Check: Students should underline "I felt he knew."

p. 110 Literary Analysis: Tristan likes to tease. Oscar doesn't like to be teased, and he is smart enough to do something about it.

p. 111 Literary Analysis: She cares very deeply about the cat and his safety. She is emotional, but tries to hide how she feels.

p. 111 Reading Check: Students should underline the sentence beginning, "We were having a meeting of the Mothers' Union. . . ."

p. 111 Stop to Reflect: Students may say that he wanted a change of scene.

p. 112 Literary Analysis: Students should underline "huge benevolent smile," "Brought your cat," "closed his eyes a few moments before articulating carefully," "Jack giggled," and "He's some cat."

p. 112 Literary Analysis: Students may say that Oscar is a happy cat who likes people, takes care of himself, and is smart.

p. 112 Reading Check: He attends an evening event.

p. 113 Stop to Reflect: Students may say that Oscar is not trying to run away because he doesn't leave town-he just goes somewhere to visit.

p. 113 Reading Strategy: Students should circle "socialite," "high stepper," and "cat-about-town." Students expressions will vary but should show Oscar is someone who likes to socialize.

p. 113 Reading Check: They don't worry about him any longer. Rather, they enjoy knowing about his visits.

p. 114 Stop to Reflect: Students may guess that the Herriots are going to lose the cat in some way.

p. 114 Literary Analysis: Students should circle "o'," "ah," "'im," "meetin's," "'ad," and "huntin'." He uses "ah" instead of I.

p. 114 Reading Check: They think he is their lost cat, who was named Tiger.

p. 115 Literary Analysis: Students may choose "The man's face seemed lit from within," "he replied happily," and "decent, honest, uncomplicated Yorkshire face." Accept other reasonable choices. Possible response: Sep Gibbons is a happy, honest, hardworking, loving man.

p. 115 Stop to Reflect: Students may say that it was a hard decision because she was very attached to the cat.
Also the words "unnatural brightness" shows that she was covering up feelings.

p. 115 Reading Check: The Gibbons family takes him with them.

p. 116 Literary Analysis: He feels very badly about giving Oscar back.

p. 116 Literary Analysis: She thinks doing the right thing is important, which is why she gave Oscar back. She didn't want the Gibbons family to feel badly, so she held her feelings in check. Here, she shows she is devastated by losing the cat.

p. 116 Reading Check: He was sad as well.

p. 117 Reading Check: They are going to visit Oscar.

p. 117 Literary Analysis: Students should underline "tableau of life with six children and thirty shillings a week," and the following sentence.

p. 117 Literary Analysis: Possible response: She's always busy, and she likes to treat company well.

p. 117 Reading Check: Oscar is out visiting.

p. 118 Literary Analysis: Students should circle "grace and majesty."

p. 118 Literary Analysis: "Ye" is used in place of "you," and "'ope" is used instead of "hope."

p. 118 Reader's Response: Students may say that they would like to have a cat like Oscar because he is such a happy, interesting, loving animal.

p. 118 Thinking About the Skill: An idiom is an expression that belongs to a particular region or language and usually does not mean the same thing as the meanings of the words that make it up.

"The Luckiest Time of All" by Lucille Clifton

p. 120 Activate Prior Knowledge: Students should describe a time they met someone by chance, then became friends.

p. 120 Literary Analysis: She means that to her and her friend, the show was so new and different that is was as marvelous as anything they would find anywhere in the world.

p. 120 Reading Check: It is a show like a circus.

p. 121 Reading Strategy: Students should underline "we run" and "runnin dog."

p. 121 Reading Check: Mr. Pickens saves her.

p. 121 Stop to Reflect: Students may say that the episode with the dog has satisfied their need for adventure.

p. 122 Reading Check: It got her acquainted with her future husband.

p. 122 Reader's Response: Students may say that they were surprised since she hit his dog with a stone.

p. 122 Thinking About the Skill: Possible response: Nearby words sometimes restate the unfamiliar word in a different way.

"How The Snake Got Poison" by Zora Neale Hurston

p. 124 Activate Prior Knowledge: Students should tell a story about how something originated.

p. 124 Literary Analysis: Students should circle "everything trods upon me and kills off my generations."

p. 124 Literary Analysis: Students should circle the sentence beginning, "He' layin' in de bushes there wid poison. . . ."

p. 124 Reading Check: The snake complains about being trampled, so God gives him poison. The varmints complain about being killed by the snake. God tells the snake he didn't mean for the snake to kill everything that moves.

p. 125 Reading Check: The snake also gets a rattle.

p. 125 Reader's Response: Possible response: I would have told the snake to hide better in the first place so others wouldn't step on him.

p. 125 Thinking About the Skill: Because he couldn't see much from below, he tended to think of everyone as his enemy. If he had stood up, he would have had a better view of who was coming and been less fearful.

Unit 6

"After Twenty Years" by O. Henry

p. 127 Activate Prior Knowledge: Students should list two ways police work is different from what it was one hundred years ago, such as police cars and police radios, improved forensics, DNA matching, finger printing, and so forth.

p. 127 Reading Strategy: Students should underline officer once and made twice. They should place vertical lines in between went and twirling, between movements and turning, between thoroughfare and the, between officer and with, and between swagger and made.

p. 127 Literary Analysis: Students should underline "When about midway of a certain block the policeman suddenly slowed his walk." This sentence hints that the policeman has seen something suspicious.

p. 128 Literary Analysis: Students should underline the sentence that begins "Well, we agreed that night . . ."

p. 128 Reading Strategy: The part of the sentence that describes Jimmy is "he always was the truest, stanchest old chap in the world."

p. 128 Reading Check: The man belittles his friend while building himself up so that he sounds great.

p. 129 Reading Strategy: Students should underline "man" and circle "smoked" and "waited." They should respond that the commas break up the sentence into manageable chunks so that the reader can look at each chunk separately to decide what it means.

p. 129 Literary Analysis: Students should underline two of the following sentences: 1) "You've changed lots, Jimmy. I never thought you were so tall by two inches." 2) "I have a position in one of the city departments." 3) "The other, submerged in his overcoat, listened with interest."

p. 129 Literary Analysis: The reader expects this man to be Jimmy Wells, but it is not.

p. 130 Literary Analysis: The surprise ending is that the tall man in the overcoat is not Jimmy Wells at all but a policeman sent by Wells to arrest the man in the doorway, who is a criminal called "Silky" Bob, wanted by the Chicago police.

p. 130 Literary Analysis: It's surprising that Jimmy was actually going to keep his twenty-year appointment with his friend and that, at the very moment of seeing him, he recognizes that his friend is a wanted criminal. It is also surprising that an occasion of reunion and happiness turns into a negative thing—an arrest.

p. 130 Stop to Reflect: Sample answer: Even though Jimmy recognized Bob as a criminal, he felt badly that his friend had turned out this way. Because of his feelings for his friend, he couldn't bear to turn him in himself. He may also have been trying to spare his friend from embarrassment. These are positive motivations.

p. 130 Reader's Response: Sample response: Yes, I think Patrolman Wells did the right thing because it was his duty as an officer of the law to arrest criminals.

p. 130 Thinking About the Skill: The foreshadowing in the story gives hints to the reader. If the reader pays attention to these hints, he or she will not be totally surprised by the ending. Students should give at least one example of foreshadowing—for example, the fact that the man hangs out in a dark doorway and feels a need to explain why he is there to the policeman indicates that he is nervous for some reason (the reader knows later that the reason he is nervous when the policeman comes is that he is a criminal).

"Rikki-tikki-tavi" by Rudyard Kipling

p. 132 Activate Prior Knowledge: Students should choose two animals that are natural enemies and give a couple of examples of how they act together.

p. 132 Literary Analysis: Sample answer: Rikki-tikki is a mongoose the size of a small cat with fur and tail like a cat's-except when the tail is fluffed up. He has a pink nose and eyes. He makes a sound like scolding.

p. 132 Literary Analysis: The major character is Rikki. The story is named after him and the exposition is all about him.

p. 133 Reading Strategy: Students should underline the sentence, "Run and find out." The motto refers to the mongoose's natural curiosity. It might cause Rikki trouble because he might "run and find out" before looking to see what danger might be there.

p. 133 Literary Analysis: The minor characters are Teddy, Teddy's father, and Teddy's mother.

p. 133 Reading Check: Rikki explores his surroundings thoroughly, almost drowning in bathtubs, burning his nose on Teddy's father's cigar, checking out all the sounds at night.

p. 133 Reading Strategy: Students might predict that the mongoose will indeed protect Teddy from a snake.

p. 134 Stop to Reflect: Like all mongooses, Rikki wants to be a house mongoose and follow in the steps his mother taught him.

p. 134 Literary Analysis: The encounter with Darzee establishes the conflict by alerting Rikki to Nag's evil ways-specifically, about Nag's eating one of their babies.

p. 134 Reading Check: Students should write these three details: 1) Nag is five feet long. 2) He has a large hood he can spread. 3) He has a mark like the eye of a hook-and-eye fastening on the back of his hood. Students should underline the phrase, ". . . the spectacle mark on the back of it that looks exactly like the eye part of a hook-and-eye fastening."

p. 135 Reading Check: Students should underline the phrase ". . . he knew that all a grown mongoose's business in life was to fight and eat snakes."

p. 135 Reading Strategy: Students might predict that Rikki and Nag will have a fight.

p. 135 Stop to Reflect: Students' answers should touch on the laws of nature and how an animal's instincts help it to survive.

p. 136 Literary Analysis: In their first encounter, while Nag talks to Rikki, Nagaina tries to kill Rikki from the rear. This encounter intensifies the conflict by establishing that the cobras and Rikki are enemies.

p. 136 Reading Check: Students should underline the following: "If Rikki-tikki had only known, he was doing a much more dangerous thing than fighting Nag, for Karait is so small, and can turn so quickly, that unless Rikki bit him close to the back of the head, he would get the return stroke in his eye or lip. But Rikki did not know . . ."

p. 136 Reading Strategy: Students might guess that the encounter with this small snake foreshadows what will happen to the cobras. It gives a clue about what might happen.

p. 137 Stop to Reflect: Sample answer: Rikki now knows he is the protector of the family. He does not overeat or indulge himself in being petted so he can stay constantly on guard.

p. 137 Reading Check: Chuchundra is consumed by fear. Students should underline three of the following phrases: "a broken-hearted little beast"; "He whimpers and cheeps all the night, trying to make up his mind to run into the middle of the room, but he never gets there"; "'Don't kill me,'" said Chuchundra, almost weeping"; "Chuchundra sat down and cried till the tears rolled off his whiskers."

p. 137 Literary Analysis: Chuchundra and Chua, the rat, know that one of the snakes is planning to go into the house. Chuchundra tells Rikki to listen. When Rikki does, he hears them plotting.

p. 138 Literary Analysis: Chuchundra is a minor character. 1) He moves the plot along but 2) he is not involved in the major action of the story.

p. 138 Reading Check: Nag and Nagaina plan to enter the house to kill Teddy and his parents. They remember that there were no mongooses in the house when there were no people there, so they think Rikki will leave after the family is dead.

p. 138 Reading Check: Students should underline the sentences, "Now, when Karait was killed, the big man had a stick. He may have that stick still, but when he comes in to bathe in the morning he will not have a stick."

p. 139 Reading Strategy: If students answer that their prediction was correct, they should back their answer up with evidence from the story.

p. 139 Literary Analysis: Sample answer: Because there are two snakes and several cobra eggs, you know that Rikki will have to deal with them, too. Therefore, the death of the first snake is a build up to the high point of the story-the ridding of the garden of all cobras.

p. 139 Reading Check: 1) Nagaina will be enraged because she knows Rikki killed Nag. 2) She will be protecting her eggs.

p. 140 Stop to Reflect: Darzee sings about Rikki's battle with Nag. Students should underline two of these details: 1) "The valiant Rikki-tikki caught him by the head and held fast." 2) "The big man brought the bang-stick and Nag fell in two pieces." 3) ". . . Nag came out on the end of a stick" 4) ". . . the sweeper picked him up on the end of a stick and threw him upon the rubbish head." They should circle two of the following: 1) "valiant Rikki-tikki" 2) "the great, the red-eyed Rikki-tikki" 3) "the great, the beautiful Rikki-tikki" 4) "O Killer of the terrible Nag"

p. 140 Reading Check: Students should underline the sentence, "You don't know when to do the right thing at the right time."

p. 140 Reading Strategy: Students' predictions should be a logical deduction of how Rikki might use the cobra eggs to help outwit Nagaina. He is mad at Darzee because, if he had known there were cobra eggs, he would have already destroyed them.

p. 141 Reading Check: Darzee's wife is trying to divert Nagaina so Rikki can get to her eggs.

p. 141 Reading Strategy: Students' answers should indicate that Rikki is going to use one of the eggs-probably to divert Nagaina.

p. 141 Literary Analysis: They do not think that Nagaina will go onto the veranda to kill the family.

p. 142 Literary Analysis: Nagaina is a major character in the story. 1) She is the main opposing force against Rikki. 2) The plot revolves around her trying to keep control of the garden.

p. 142 Literary Analysis: The action of the story is speeding up. Rikki is enticing Nagaina to fight him. The fight will determine who controls the garden.

p. 142 Stop to Reflect: Rikki boasts to Nagaina about his defeat of Nag to make her upset before they fight so that she might make a mistake.

p. 142 Reading Strategy: If their response is positive, students should tell how their prediction is a match with what really happens. When Rikki tells Nagaina that the egg in his mouth is the last one, she lunges for it, allowing Teddy's father to grab him out of harm's way.

p. 143 Reading Strategy: Students' predictions should take into account what has already taken place in the story.

p. 143 Reading Check: Again, Darzee's wife is being helpful by trying to divert Nagaina from going into the hole with her egg.

p. 143 Literary Analysis: Students should underline this passage: "It is all over," he said. "The widow will never come out again."

p. 144 Literary Analysis: Students should underline three of the following: 1) "And the red ants that live between the grass stems heard him, and began to troop down one after another to see if he had spoken the truth." 2) "Rikki-tikki curled himself up in the grass and slept where he was . . ." 3) ". . . he heard his 'attention' notes like a tiny dinner gong; and then the steady 'Ding-dong-tock! Nag is dead-dong! Nagaina is dead! Ding-dong-tock!'" 4) ". . . Teddy and Teddy's mother and Teddy's father came out and almost cried over him . . ." 5) "That night he ate all that was given him . . ." 6) ". . . went to bed on Teddy's shoulder . . ." For the resolution, students should circle ". . . he kept the garden as a mongoose should keep it, with tooth and jump and spring and bite, till never a cobra dared show its head inside the walls." It is the resolution because Rikki now has control of the garden.

p. 144 Stop to Reflect: Sample answer: No, Rikki is being quite matter-of-fact about his accomplishments and his abilities.

p. 144 Reader's Response: Sample answer: Kipling wants to leave the battle to the reader's imagination. Also, having Rikki appear-alive-after Darzee is already singing his death song makes this scene more dra-

matic. Students should also state whether they liked the ending or not.

p. 144 Thinking About the Skill: Students' answers should show an understanding of the skill they have chosen and give at least one example of why it has been helpful.

"Papa's Parrot" by Cynthia Rylant

p. 146 Activate Prior Knowledge: If possible, students should give real examples from their own lives of what happens to people who have suffered heart attacks, such as hospital stay, by-pass surgery, death, decreased mobility, and so forth.

p. 146 Literary Analysis: Students should underline the following: 1) "Mr. Tillian looked forward to seeing his son and his son's friends ever day." 2) "He liked the company."

p. 146 Reading Strategy: Sample answer: I would be embarrassed if my father talked to a parrot, too. My friends might think my dad was weird-or they might think I was weird for having a dad like that.

p. 147 Literary Analysis: Students should underline three of the following details: 1) "Mr. Tillian couldn't leave the hospital." 2) "He lay in bed, tubes in his arms . . ." 3) ". . . he worried about his shop." 4) "Rocky would be hungry."

p. 147 Stop to Reflect: Harry might think the store seems strange without his father there.

p. 147 Literary Analysis: 1) Harry calls Rocky a name. He is not nice to the parrot because he does not like how his father interacts with the parrot. 2) Harry cleans Rocky's cage, fills his food and water dishes, and sorts the candy. He is responsible.

p. 148 Reading Check: The parrot is imitating what he has heard Harry's father say so often.

p. 148 Literary Analysis: His reaction 1) shows that he really loves his father and 2) that he realizes how poorly he has treated him.

p. 148 Literary Analysis: It is an example of indirect characterization because the writer is showing Harry's feelings.

p. 148 Reading Strategy: Students' responses should be honest reactions to Harry's shame and sadness about neglecting his father.

p. 148 Reader's Response: Sample answer: Yes, I think the realization of how Harry has neglected his father will make him visit the shop more, be nicer about Rocky, and perhaps even help out in the shop.

p. 148 Thinking About the Skill: Sample answer: Figuring out things by yourself-through reading the characters' words and thoughts and seeing their actions-is usually more satisfying than being told things directly. You put something more into your reading through indirect characterization. Reading becomes an active rather than a passive process.

"Ribbons" by Laurence Yep

p. 150 Activate Prior Knowledge: Students' descriptions should include examples of the differences in the two cultures and an explanation of what students learned from the experience.

p. 150 Literary Analysis: Students might suggest one of these themes: 1) the older generation interacting with the younger; 2) learning from cultural differences; 3) having to give up something meaningful to you for someone else; or 4) the bonds the occur in families.

p. 150 Reading Strategy: Students might ask questions such as: 1) How will the girl react to having to give up her ballet lessons? 2) How will the grandchildren get along with their grandmother? 3) What's it like to have a relative living in your home? 4) Will life be different living with someone from a different culture?

p. 151 Reading Strategy: Students should underline the sentence, "But what happened to them?" 1) Sample answer: Yes, it would be a good question to ask about the story. 2) Sample answer: Perhaps Stacy's mother doesn't tell her because the grandmother does not want her to. 3) Sample answer: The writer might want to build suspense in the story, or he might feel that telling Stacy now would ruin the story.

p. 151 Reading Strategy: Students should underline the following: 1) "However, when I tried to put my arms around her and kiss her, she stiffened in surprise. "Nice children don't drool on people," she snapped at me." 2) "Grandmother didn't even thank me." Sample answer: I'm sure Stacy's grandmother's treatment of her will affect her attitude in a negative way.

p. 152 Stop to Reflect: Sample answer: This information about the grandmother makes me feel more kindly towards her and admire her.

p. 152 Reading Check: The belongings look and smell foreign and exotic, causing Stacy to imagine what Hong Kong is like. She unconsciously starts to dance to express her imaginings.

p. 152 Literary Analysis: Sample answer: The passage suggests a theme of conflict that arises when a household changes, especially when there is a mix of young and old people or when new people are added to the household.

p. 153 Reading Strategy: Sample question: Why does the grandmother seem to like and treat Ian better than she does Stacy?

p. 153 Literary Analysis: The passage relates to the theme that people from different cultures have different customs that can make understanding each other difficult.

p. 153 Reading Strategy: Sample answer: Does the grandmother sometimes feel like a "freak" just as Stacy does because they both feel out of place in the American culture?

p. 153 Reading Check: Students should underline, "And, I thought in a flash, the best way to know a person is to know what she loves. For me, that was ballet."

p. 154 Reading Strategy: Sample question: Why does the grandmother hate Stacy's toe-shoe ribbons so much?

p. 154 Stop to Reflect: Neither Stacy nor her grandmother seems to understand the other. Stacy's mother, however, understands the customs of both cultures.

p. 154 Literary Analysis: Stacy's mother's statement relates to the theme that people from different cultures have different customs that makes understanding each other difficult.

p. 154 Reading Check: Students should underline the following: "Can't you see how worked up Paw-paw is?" she whispered. "She won't listen to reasons. Give her some time. Let her cool off."

p. 155 Reading Check: Students should underline the sentence, "'She associates them with something awful that happened to her,' Mom said." They should circle the sentence, "She made me promise never to talk about it to anyone."

p. 155 Reading Strategy: Sample question: Will Stacy's decision help or hurt her relationship with her grandmother?

p. 155 Stop to Reflect: Her grandmother is ashamed of her feet and is upset that Stacy has seen them. Her feelings cause her to act gruffly.

p. 155 Literary Analysis: Stacy's mom explains a former custom of China to try to help Stacy understand her grandmother, so the theme is understanding people from other cultures.

p. 156 Reading Check: Stacy finally figures out that her grandmother mistakes Stacy's toe-shoe ribbons for the ribbons that were used to bind her feet.

p. 156 Stop to Reflect: Sample answer: Stacy's grandmother loves Stacy; she has just had a series of unfortunate incidents with her. Her treatment of Stacy changes; she begins to ignore Stacy because of her embarrassment about her feet.

p. 156 Reading Strategy: Sample answer: Will reading this story together begin to heal the problems between Stacy and her grandmother?

p. 157 Reading Check: 1) The grandmother is really talking about herself, not the mermaid. 2) The situations of the mermaid and the grandmother are somewhat similar. 3) The grandmother is trying to tell Stacy indirectly something about her own life.

p. 157 Stop to Reflect: The grandmother was trying to protect Stacy from pain because she loves her.

p. 157 Literary Analysis: The ties of family love are very strong and can overcome misunderstanding and other problems.

p. 157 Reader's Response: Students may say that they would have explained what the ballet ribbons were for to the grandmother.

p. 157 Thinking About the Skill: Sample answer: Asking questions makes you think about the story more and allows you to have deeper insights into it. For example, if you ask why the grandmother hates Stacy's toe-shoe ribbons, you begin to look for or guess at answers instead of just thinking the grandmother is mean and unfair.

"The Treasure of Lemon Brown" by Walter Dean Myers

p. 159 Activate Prior Knowledge: Students' descriptions should tell what they learned from an older individual.

p. 159 Reading Strategy: Sample questions: 1) Why doesn't Greg's father understand the importance of baseball in Greg's life? 2) Why hasn't Greg spent more time trying to improve his math grade? 3) How would Greg react to his father's discussion of his own hardships? 4) Is there another way Greg's father could have communicated his disappointment in Greg's performance in math?

p. 159 Literary Analysis: Sample answer: One theme of the story could be getting along in families; another could be younger people learning from older ones.

p. 160 Reading Strategy: The writer wants you to know that this neighborhood is somewhat run-down.

p. 160 Literary Analysis: Students should underline the sentence, "His father had been a postal worker for all Greg's life, and was proud of it, often telling Greg how hard he had worked to pass the test." This sentence might point to a theme of pride in one's work, especially if it is hard work.

p. 160 Stop to Reflect: Students' answers should indicate that they would probably be frightened because they couldn't see anything and didn't know whose voice they could hear.

p. 161 Reading Strategy: You might ask, "Why does the new character say this?"

p. 161 Reading Check: Students should underline three of these details: 1) ". . . an old man with a wrinkled face . . ." 2) ". . . crinkly white hair . . ." 3) ". . . whiskers . . ." 4) ". . . dirty coats piled on his smallish frame . . ." 5) "His pants were bagged to the knee . . ." 6) ". . . rags that went down to the old shoes. . . . The rags were held on with strings . . ." 7) ". . . there was a rope around his middle."

p. 161 Reading Check: He relaxes because he knows this man and knows that he is harmless.

p. 162 Reading Strategy: You might ask, "What treasure could this man possibly have?"

p. 162 Literary Analysis: Sample answer: He means that every person has something that is the most important thing to him or her. A possible theme might be that love and family are more important than material things.

p. 162 Literary Analysis: Lemon Brown is very matter-of-fact in his attitude about his hard times. He indicates that hard times are just an ordinary part of life.

p. 163 Reading Strategy: Sample questions: 1) "Who are these men?" 2) "Do they mean to injure Lemon Brown?" 3) "What will these two defenseless people do against them?"

p. 163 Literary Analysis: Sample answer: Lemon Brown probably squeezes Greg's hand to give him courage, which would relate to a theme of older people caring and feeling responsibility for younger people.

p. 163 Stop to Reflect: They are probably planning to steal his treasure from him.

p. 164 Reading Strategy: You would read on to see what happens.

p. 164 Reading Strategy: Why is Lemon Brown letting the men know where he is?

p. 164 Reading Check: Students should underline the sentence, "He swallowed hard, wet his lips once more and howled as evenly as he could." He howls to try to scare the men.

p. 164 Literary Analysis: Greg is showing concern for Lemon Brown. They have experienced something difficult together, which has created a bond between them. The theme would be the importance of mutual care between people of different generations.

p. 165 Literary Analysis: Lemon Brown's attitude is to meet pain and other problems head on and as if they aren't new because then they won't bother you. His sense of humor also helps him.

p. 165 Reading Check: The sentence is, "He revealed some yellowed newspaper clippings and a battered harmonica."

p. 165 Literary Analysis: Sample answer: A person's treasure is those things important to him as a person, not expensive objects that have no meaning.

p. 166 Reading Check: Students should underline these two sentences: 1) "Him carrying it around with him like that told me it meant something to him." 2) "That was my treasure, and when I give it to him he treated it just like that, a treasure."

p. 166 Reading Strategy: Sample questions: 1) How does Lemon Brown feel about Greg? 2) Is Lemon Brown joking with Greg about not knowing anything or is Lemon Brown being serious? 3) Why does Lemon Brown challenge Greg when Greg says, "I guess so"?

p. 166 Literary Analysis: Lemon Brown downplays his affection for Greg, but this affection relates to the theme of the older generation watching out and caring for the younger one.

p. 166 Stop to Reflect: Students' answers should show an understanding of the story and its themes.

p. 167 Reading Strategy: Sample questions: 1) What will Greg's father do when he gets home? 2) Why does Greg decide not to tell his father about Lemon Brown? 3) Why does he think Lemon Brown will be all right?

p. 167 Literary Analysis: Sample answer: Greg smiles because he knows his attitude will be different now after his experience with Lemon Brown. In other words, he will change his behavior so he won't need the lecture. This attitude shows that he has learned some new ideas of how to be from this older, experienced person-a theme of the story.

p. 167 Reader's Response: Sample answer: Yes, Greg has learned a lot about hard work, being responsible, family connections, and what's important in life from Lemon Brown. I think I would try to change just as Greg is going to.

p. 167 Thinking About the Skill: Sample answer: Thinking about what the themes of the story might be has helped me look more deeply into the story. I have gained more insights by doing so and now understand that stories are written for more than entertainment; they also allow people to think about important life issues.

Unit 7

"How To Enjoy Poetry" by James Dickey

p. 169 Activate Prior Knowledge: Students should list three characteristics of one of their school supplies.

p. 169 Literary Analysis: Students should underline the last sentence of the first paragraph.

p. 169 Reading Strategy: Possible response: The first section says that words and things, actions, and feelings go together. The second section says that you have to reach out to poetry to make a connection.

p. 169 Reading Check: The reader's job is to reach out to the poem.

p. 170 Reading Strategy: Students should underline "It should bypass all classrooms, all textbooks, courses, examinations, and libraries" and circle either "go straight to the things that make your own existence exist" or the sentence beginning "Find your own way . . . to open yourself. . . ."

p. 170 Stop to Reflect: Students should choose one thing from the list and write the image it evokes.

p. 171 Reading Strategy: Students should underline the sentence beginning "Almost anything put into rhythm . . ."

p. 171 Stop to Reflect: He wants to encourage people to write poetry.

p. 171 Reading Check: He compares writing poetry to having a contest with yourself.

p. 172 Stop to Reflect: He wants people to understand how much there is to gain from reading and writing poetry.

p. 172 Reader's Response: Students may say that they want to read or write poetry to learn more about themselves and the world.

p. 172 Thinking About the Skill: Students may say that it helped them organize the information so they could remember it more clearly.

"The Chase from An American Childhood" by Annie Dillard

p. 174 Activate Prior Knowledge: Students should tell of a time they gave everything they had to an activity.

p. 174 Reading Strategy: To succeed at something, you have to throw yourself into it fully.

p. 174 Reading Check: They like to throw snowballs at cars.

p. 175 Reading Check: They each threw a snowball at the car.

p. 175 Reading Strategy: She wants the reader to really experience the thrill of the chase, so she describes it as completely and accurately as possible.

p. 175 Reading Check: The driver gets out of the car and starts to chase them.

p. 176 Stop to Reflect: He knows that you have to fling yourself at what you are doing.

p. 176 Literary Analysis: Students should underline "I was cherishing my excitement."

p. 176 Reading Check: He chases them for ten blocks.

p. 177 Literary Analysis: Students should circle "redundant," "a mere formality," or "beside the point."

p. 177 Stop to Reflect: She has done something that required her to use everything she had and is thrilled from the effort.

p. 177 Reader's Response: Many students will say they would like to have her as a friend because she would be fun to be with—enthusiastic and positive.

p. 177 Thinking About the Skill: She thinks that you need to throw yourself completely into something to get the full reward of the activity.

"I Am a Native of North America" by Chief Dan George

p. 179 Activate Prior Knowledge: Students may suggest goals around ending hunger, cleaning up the environment, or ending crime.

p. 179 Reading Strategy: Students should circle any three details in the paragraph except the last sentence.

p. 179 Reading Check: He was born into a Native culture.

p. 180 Literary Analysis: Students should underline the sentence beginning "This is why I find it hard. . . ."

p. 180 Reading Strategy: Students should mention stripping the hills, tearing things from the earth, throwing poison in the water, and choking the air with fumes.

p. 180 Literary Analysis: Students should circle "need" and "must." The essay was written to persuade people because he is trying to convince the reader using strong words.

p. 181 Literary Analysis: His Native culture respected people and the Earth. White culture separates people, treats the earth badly, and is lacking in love.

p. 181 Reading Check: He describes brotherhood as a love that forgives and forgets and shares trust and acceptance.

p. 181 Reader's Response: Possible response: The power to love is the most important quality because without it people become isolated and bitter.

"All Together Now" by Barbara Jordan

p. 183 Activate Prior Knowledge: Students should tell about a friend who was different and what they gained from the relationship.

p. 183 Reading Strategy: Students should underline the sentence beginning "President Lyndon B. Johnson . . ." and the following sentence.

p. 183 Literary Analysis: Students should underline "As our society becomes more diverse, people of all races and backgrounds will have to learn to live together."

p. 183 Reading Check: The essay is about improving race relations.

p. 184 Literary Analysis: Students should underline the sentence beginning "Each of us can decide to have one friend. . . ."

p. 184 Reading Check: She says that babies are not born racist, but that they have to adopt racist attitudes.

p. 184 Stop to Reflect: Both authors believe in the power of love.

p. 184 Reader's Response: Students may say that they hadn't realized that just making a friend from a different group would make a difference.

p. 184 Thinking About the Skill: Students may say that she backed up her statements with facts, and so did give enough support.

Unit 8

"A Christmas Carol: Scrooge and Marley" Dramatized by Israel Horovitz (Adapted from Charles Dickens)

Act I, Scenes 1 & 2

p. 186 Activate Prior Knowledge: Students' descriptions of their experiences should include details. They should explain why this experience was so important in developing their character or attitudes.

p. 186 Stop to Reflect: In a play like "A Christmas Carol," where there are many characters, a list of characters helps you keep them straight. You can flip back at any time to see that, for instance, Fred is Scrooge's nephew.

p. 187 Literary Analysis: Students should circle, "Ghostly music . . . out to the auditorium." Because readers can't see things like lighting effects and the actors like an audience can, they need to be told what they would see if they were actually at the play.

p. 187 Reading Strategy: Students should underline three of the following: "frozen features," "pointed nose," "red eyes," "blue thin lips"; sound of his voice: "grating voice"; way he walks: "stiffened gait."

p. 187 Literary Analysis: Students should circle "Downstage Center."

p. 188 Literary Analysis: You see by the dialogue that Scrooge is more interested in money than in people's lives and hardships. Marley is disgusted with Scrooge—his lack of any true feelings about his business partner, Marley; his stinginess; his disagreeableness as evidenced by the fact that no one will approach him in the street to even ask a question. Therefore, Marley either must not have been as bad as Scrooge, or death has changed him into a nicer person.

p. 188 Reading Check: Students' rewriting of the sentence should indicate that Scrooge had few dealings with his fellow man.

p. 188 Literary Analysis: Explosions accompanied by puffs of smoke would make Marley's entrances and exits more mysterious and ghostly.

p. 189 Reading Strategy: Students should underline "tiny fire," "door is open and in his line of vision . . . Bob Cratchit," "dismal tank of a cubicle," "fire so tiny as to barely cast a light," "white comforter," "candle."

p. 189 Literary Analysis: Sample answer: The dialogue tells the reader that the nephew values the intent behind Christmas-love and unselfishness towards others-and Scrooge does not. The dialogue also contrasts the cheerfulness of the nephew with the grumpiness of his uncle.

p. 189 Stop to Reflect: It appears that the nephew keeps trying to have a positive relationship with his uncle, but Scrooge doesn't seem to care. People's personalities are what they themselves create and are not genetically inherited.

p. 190 Literary Analysis: The stage direction tells the reader that Cratchit agrees with the nephew, not with Scrooge.

p. 190 Reading Check: Students should underline the sentence, "Let me hear another sound from you and you'll keep your Christmas by losing your situation."

p. 190 Stop to Reflect: Sample answer: Scrooge thinks love is ridiculous. Perhaps he feels negatively about love because he had an unhappy experience with it.

p. 190 Reading Check: The nephew is saying that he is sorry his uncle is so determined to hate Christmas and that he has made the attempt to invite him to Christmas dinner as part of "keeping" the Christmas spirit.

p. 191 Reading Check: Cratchit is being emphatic in his agreement with the nephew about the right spirit of Christmas. Scrooge responds by grouping the two men together and making fun of their love of a holiday when neither of them has very much money.

p. 191 Reading Strategy: Students should underline three of the following: "DO-GOODERS," "portly," "thin," "pleasant."

p. 191 Reading Check: The portly man indicates that Marley was generous. He makes the assumption that Scrooge, therefore, is also generous.

p. 192 Literary Analysis: Sample answer: Life was very difficult for the poor. The portly man's attitude indicates that the places and things Scrooge mentions—the prisons, the workhouses, the Treadmill, and "Poor Law"—are terrible.

p. 192 Reading Check: Students should underline "What shall I put you down for, sir?" and "You wish to be left anonymous?"

p. 192 Literary Analysis: Scrooge thinks that the poor are none of his business and that he shouldn't interfere with them.

p. 192 Reading Strategy: Sample answer: Shock and surprise are probably on the faces of the two men.

p. 193 Stop to Reflect: Sample answer: Cratchit gives the thin man some money. This action tells the reader that Cratchit, although poor, is also generous and does not want to be put in the same category with Scrooge.

p. 193 Reading Check: Scrooge is saying that to pay for a day Cratchit does not work, even though it is holiday that everybody gets off, is not fair and like "picking his pocket"—stealing from him.

p. 193 Literary Analysis: Scrooge reaffirms his miserliness and lack of generosity towards people.

p. 194 Stop to Reflect: Cratchit is so full of good will that he almost can't help saying "Merry Christmas." Also, he doesn't base his behavior on Scrooge's but does what he thinks is right.

p. 194 Literary Analysis: Students should underline the sentence, "This statement of Scrooge's character, by contrast to all other characters, should seem comical to the audience." The writer says that this should be accomplished by contrast; that is, all the other characters should be happy, enjoying the snow, whereas Scrooge will be grumpy, batting at the snowflakes and snapping at people.

p. 194 Reading Strategy: The stage directions are quite detailed about how both Scrooge and the other characters in this scene should act, so you can see quite easily the pleasant winter scene with Scrooge as the one detractor.

p. 194 Reader's Response: Sample answer: The writer wants to make sure the reader sees few, if any, redeemable characteristics in Scrooge in order to prepare the reader for what comes next. Students may answer that they are sorry for Scrooge because he is such an unpleasant person, nobody likes him, and he is unhappy all the time.

p. 194 Thinking About the Skill: Being able to picture a scene in your mind is especially helpful in a play because a play depends on action, or events being acted out for you. Thus, being able to read about a scene puts a reader on equal footing with a playgoer who actually sees the play.

Act I, Scenes 4 & 5

p. 196 Activate Prior Knowledge: Students' examples should tell how the ghost they chose functions in the story. Sample example: In Hamlet, Hamlet's father's ghost comes to tell him that his brother, Hamlet's uncle, killed him and then married his wife, Hamlet's mother, so that Hamlet will seek revenge.

p. 196 Literary Analysis: Students should mention two of the following: 1) children are singing a carol 2) Scrooge is asleep, "dead to the world" 3) Marley comes into view. It is important to explain the stage set-up so the reader knows that the stage is split by the scrim to separate the outdoors from the inside.

p. 196 Literary Analysis: Students should underline the sentence, "From this point forth . . . I shall be quite visible to you, but invisible to him."

p. 196 Stop to Reflect: Students should underline "I cannot in any way afford to lose my days. Securities come due, promissory notes, interest on investments: these are things that happen in the daylight!" Scrooge still seems centered on money and business.

p. 197 Reading Check: Scrooge is paying close attention to the time because he was told by Marley's ghost that the ghosts would begin appearing at 1 o'clock.

p. 197 Literary Analysis: It is important for the reader to be able to picture the ghost since he or she can't see it like a person watching the play could.

p. 197 Stop to Reflect: Students' answers should indicate that they might be afraid because it's a ghost or not afraid because they were warned.

p. 198 Literary Analysis: The stage directions indicate the change of scene.

p. 198 Stop to Reflect: The audience can see Marley, but Scrooge can't. Marley tells the audience (the reader, too) that, for the first time in a long time, Scrooge is awakening to life and feelings and is beginning to change.

p. 198 Reading Check: To be "stagnant" means "without motion"; therefore, Scrooge means he can't bear to stay in this place.

p. 198 Reading Strategy: Students should write two of the following: 1) The stage directions help you picture Scrooge weeping and staggering around; 2) Scrooge's details of the scenery and the use of the pronoun "my" let you know how important they are to him. 3) The use of exclamation marks lets you know how excited Scrooge is, which you could tell if you were watching the play by the acting.

p. 199 Literary Analysis: Sample answer: This scene helps the reader figure out that being alone was a usual part of Scrooge's childhood and that being alone may have become the most familiar way for him to be as an adult-whether he wanted aloneness or not.

p. 199 Stop to Reflect: Sample answer: Remembering his own lonely experience as a boy allows Scrooge to relate to the singing boy. He is beginning to think of other people and have empathy for them.

p. 199 Reading Strategy: Again, the reader has an image of aloneness, but this time it is broken by the entrance of a younger girl about six years old.

p. 199 Reading Check: Scrooge's home life must have been very unhappy. It sounds as if his father was unkind to him and sent him away to school because he didn't want him around.

p. 200 Reading Check: 1) The Schoolmaster ignores Fan when Scrooge tries to introduce her. 2) Fan grabs the Schoolmaster's coattail and insists that he say goodbye to her brother. 3) It is clear that Scrooge has not been happy in such an unpleasant, unkind environment.

p. 200 Literary Analysis: The dialogue shows how spunky Fan is, especially for a young child, and how much she loves her brother and hates to see him ill-treated.

p. 200 Reading Strategy: The stage directions describe Fan's actions-bursting into the room, grabbing the Schoolmaster's coattail, smiling, curtseying, and lowering her eyes like a lady-and the Schoolmaster's amazed reaction to her, as well as his final handshake with Scrooge.

p. 201 Reading Strategy: The action of this scene shows the people dancing and having fun. Nothing they are saying to each other is important in the plot of the play. If there were no stage directions, the reader would have no idea that this scene even took place.

p. 201 Stop to Reflect: The Ghost of Christmas Past wanted to show Scrooge an earlier, happier time in his past when Christmas, good will, and relationships with people were important to him.

p. 202 Reading Check: Students should underline the following: "Fezziwig had the power to make us happy or unhappy; to make our service light or burdensome; a pleasure or a toil. The happiness he gave is quite as great as if it cost him a fortune."

p. 202 Reading Check: Scrooge has realized what an ungenerous, mean employer he has been.

p. 202 Stop to Reflect: The woman means that the pursuit of wealth has become more important to Scrooge than she is. People worship an idol.

p. 203 Reading Strategy: The characters are having an argument about their engagement and their future. Neither is forceful or angry, but the woman is likely passionate about what she says.

p. 203 Reading Check: 1) She releases him from their engagement. 2) His nature has changed so much from what it had been when they became engaged—so concentrated on wealth—that she no longer wants to marry him. 3) She doesn't think he would ask her to marry him now because she has little money.

p. 203 Stop to Reflect: Sample answer: No, she is not correct; Scrooge continues to love her much longer. The rest of the scene shows how Scrooge, even in the present, wishes he were still with her. The older Scrooge tries to get the younger Scrooge to stop her and calls him a fool for not trying.

p. 204 Literary Analysis: The directions show Scrooge all alone again, unsteadily going to bed. They also indicate he has kept the cap he had as a child, which might indicate his trying to hold on to a happier time.

p. 204 Stop to Reflect: Sample answer: The Christmas Present specter will probably show Christmas with the people Scrooge knows in the present, such as his nephew and Bob Cratchit. The Christmas Future might show him horrible things about his future, like his dying, since Marley told him that a terrible fate would happen to him if he didn't heed the specters' warning.

p. 204 Reader's Response: Students might say, that they would have been upset by recalling sad memories or would have been happy by remembering some memories. They might also say they were looking forward to or were afraid of the visits of the other specters.

p. 204 Thinking About the Skills: Sample answer: Learning to picture scenes in your mind would be just as helpful in a short story or novel as it would be in a play.

Unit 9

"The Cremation of Sam McGee" by Robert Service

p. 206 Activate Prior Knowledge: Students may disagree and say that they have met people being human when conditions are not so difficult.

p. 206 Literary Analysis: Students should circle "midnight sun," "Arctic trails," "Northern Lights," "marge of Lake Lebarge," "'round the Pole," and "land of gold."

p. 206 Reading Strategy: Both can give the feeling of being stabbed.

p. 206 Reading Check: He is always cold.

p. 207 Reading Strategy: Students should circle "chilled clean through to the bone."

p. 207 Reading Check: He promises to cremate his friend.

p. 207 Literary Analysis: The cold and difficulty of building a big enough fire will make it a challenge to cremate his friend.

p. 208 Literary Analysis: He separates one word into syllables to strengthen the rhythm.

p. 208 Stop to Reflect: He may have been sweating because of how uncomfortable he felt setting his friend's body on fire.

p. 209 Reading Strategy: Students should circle "they danced about."

p. 209 Literary Analysis: He finds the wreck of a boat. sets it on fire, and burns his friend in the blaze.

p. 209 Literary Analysis: Students may say that it is a fitting ending, providing a kind of bookend to close the tale.

p. 209 Reader's Response: Most students will express surprise and delight at the poem's humorous ending.

p. 209 Thinking About the Skill: Students may say that the poem had more richness when they paid attention to its figures of speech.

"Annabel Lee" by Edgar Allan Poe

p. 211 Activate Prior Knowledge: Students should describe someone they love.

p. 211 Literary Analysis: Students should

circle "sea," "Lee," and "me" in both stanzas. The pattern is regular.

p. 211 Reading Check: She has died.

p. 212 Reading Strategy: Our love was much stronger than the love of older and wiser people. Not even angels or demons can separate my soul from Annabel Lee's.

p. 212 Literary Analysis: Students should circle "moon," "beams," "bring-," "dreams," "beau-," "Ann-," "Lee," "stars," "rise," "see," "eyes," "beau-," "Ann-," and "Lee." The rhythm is regular.

p. 212 Reader's Response: Students may say that the repetition is musical and the sad tale is moving, so the poem would make a good song.

p. 212 Thinking About the Skill: Students may say that the repetition of her name makes it clear the speaker will never forget Annabel Lee, and the regularity of the repetition suggests waves or heartbeats.

"Maestro" by Pat Mora

p. 214 Activate Prior Knowledge: Students should describe a happy memory.

p. 214 Literary Analysis: Students should circle "strummed."

p. 214 Reading Check: He hears his mother's voice.

p. 214 Reader's Response: Students are likely to say that they would like to know a family that seems so loving and supportive.

p. 214 Thinking About the Skill: Students may say that they enjoyed the "sound effects" created by onomatopoeic words.

"The Village Blacksmith" by Henry Wadsworth Longfellow

p. 216 Activate Prior Knowledge: Students should list three qualities they admire in an acquaintance.

p. 216 Literary Analysis: Students should circle "Like a sexton ringing the village bell."

p. 216 Reading Check: He has strong arms and tough, big hands; wiry, long black hair; and his face is tanned.

p. 217 Reading Strategy: He is using his sense of hearing.

p. 217 Stop to Reflect: How our lives turn out depends on the work we put into them and how we respond to life determines who we truly are.

p. 217 Reader's Response: Some students may say they admire the blacksmith for his honest approach to work and life.

p. 217 Thinking About the Skill: Possible response: The description of the smith appeals visually, the description of him swinging his sledge appeals to your sense of hearing, and the image of the flaming forge appeals to sight. (Accept any answers containing sensory images.)

Unit 10

"Popocatepetl and Ixtlaccihuatl" by Julie Piggott

p. 219 Activate Prior Knowledge: Students should tell how the story explains how a certain geological feature came into being, such as the Grand Canyon being formed when Paul Bunyan dragged his axe along the ground.

p. 219 Reading Strategy: They thought the emperor was unwise because he wouldn't allow his daughter to marry.

p. 219 Reading Check: They are volcanoes.

p. 220 Reading Check: One of the volcanoes has the same name as the princess.

p. 220 Reading Strategy: Students should underline the sentence, "This is why there were some who doubted the wisdom of the Emperor for, by not allowing his heiress to marry, he showed a selfishness and short-sightedness towards his daughter and his empire which many considered not truly wise."

p. 220 Reading Strategy: They cannot marry because the emperor has forbidden Ixtla to marry anyone.

p. 221 Reading Check: Students should underline: 1) "At last the Emperor realized himself that he was great no longer, that his power was nearly gone and that his domain was in dire peril." 2) "At last he understood that, unless his enemies were frustrated in their efforts to enter and lay waste to Tenochtitlan, not only would he no longer be Emperor but his daughter would never be Empress."

p. 221 Reading Strategy: 1) The bribe he offers to whoever lifts the siege is his daughter's hand in marriage. 2) The Emperor would cease to be Emperor.

p. 221 Stop to Reflect: Sample answer: It seems unfair for the Emperor to refuse to let Ixtla get married for years and then switch the rule so she might have to marry someone other than the man she loves.

p. 222 Literary Analysis: You can tell that these are people used to being involved in war and that their weapons are quite well developed.

p. 222 Stop to Reflect: They are probably jealous because Popo has so many good qualities: his strength, good looks, bravery. And now he is going to get the girl.

p. 222 Reading Check: Students should underline "They reached the capital . . . and quickly let it be known that . . . the warrior Popo had been killed in battle.

p. 223 Stop to Reflect: The emperor is unwise to bring up the whole issue of who Ixtla's husband will be just after he announces Popo's death. He is being insensitive to her feelings. If he cares about her enough to have her rule his kingdom, he should care about her enough to have sympathy for her. He also doesn't think about what she might do with this information.

p. 223 Reading Strategy: Ixtla loves Popo so much that she decides to marry only him. The bleakness of a future without him makes her get sick enough to die.

p. 223 Literary Analysis: The warriors' fate tells you that the culture believes in instant punishment-the death penalty-for such things as lying. The culture also allows revenge by an individual, not just an official death through the government.

p. 224 Literary Analysis: Sample answer: Because legends explain natural features, I think the two pyramids will turn into the mountains, Ixtlaccihuatl and Popocatepetl.

p. 224 Reading Strategy: The two pyramids are in the same spot as the mountains; the taller pyramid/mountain is Popocatepetl; the smoke from the torch is represented by the volcanic smoke of the mountain; the pyramids become snowcapped like the mountains.

p. 224 Reader's Response: Sample answer: Even if I had loved Ixtla, I would have found a way to get over it rather than wasting my life. I think Popo overreacts to her death (although I feel sorry for him).

"The People Could Fly" by Virginia Hamilton

p. 226 Activate Prior Knowledge: Sample answer: The song "Go Down Moses" talks about a champion coming to free the Israelites from the Egyptian pharaoh.

p. 226 Literary Analysis: Students should circle the word "standin."

p. 226 Reading Strategy: They believed in magic.

p. 227 Stop to Reflect: Sample answer: I would feel terrible and horrified when the Driver whipped a defenseless baby. The Driver was either just naturally cruel or felt that whipping people was his job so he had to do it. In which case, the Overseer or Owner, the one who set the rules, is the cruel one.

p. 227 Literary Analysis: Students should underline, 1) "Kum . . . yali, kum buba tambe," and more magic words . . ." and 2) "She flew clumsily at first . . ." or "Say she rose just as free as a bird."

p. 227 Reading Check: Students should underline "She flew over the fences. She flew over the woods. She flew like an eagle now, until she was gone from sight." Students should circle the sentence, "But it was, because they that was there saw that it was."

p. 228 Reading Check: Students should circle "Kum kunka yali, kum . . . tambe!"

p. 228 Reading Strategy: Toby laughs because he knows he has magical power and that the Master can do nothing to him.

p. 228 Reading Strategy: Freedom is the thing the slaves valued and wanted most.

p. 229 Literary Analysis: Sample answer: The message is that it is important to keep alive the hope for freedom.

p. 229 Literary Analysis: Students should underline these two sentences, 1) "When they sat close before the fire in the free land, they told it. They did so love firelight and Free-dom, and tellin." 2) "They say that the children of the ones who could not fly told their children. And now, me, I have told it to you."

p. 229 Reader's Response: Students' replies should indicate an understanding of the story, including positive reactions to flying, and perhaps sadness for those left behind (or generous feelings of happiness for those who had escaped).

p. 229 Thinking About the Skill: Sample answer: Thinking about the people's values of freedom and power and magic make me think that the story is something more than just a magical tale. It also makes me feel more strongly about the injustice that these people suffered and why freedom would be so important to them.

"Demeter and Persephone" by Anne Terry White

p. 231 Activate Prior Knowledge: The myths students choose should describe an aspect of nature explained by the myth.

p. 231 Literary Analysis: Students should underline "the gods," "giants," "monsters," and "Pluto, the king of the underworld."

p. 231 Literary Analysis: Students should underline the words "grim" and "stern."

p. 231 Reading Strategy: Students may predict that Pluto will abduct her.

p. 232 Literary Analysis: Two elements of a myth are that 1) Pluto hits the bank of the river with his trident and the earth opens; 2) the earth opens and swallows the horses, chariot, Pluto, and Persephone.

p. 232 Reading Strategy: Students might suggest that since Demeter is the goddess of the harvest, she will do something that affects the harvest.

p. 232 Reading Strategy: Students should underline three of the following: 1) "the cattle died," 2) "the seed would not come up," 3) "There was too much sun." 4) "There was too much rain." 5) "Thistles and weeds were the only things that grew."

p. 232 Reading Check: Zeus sends the gods and goddesses to plead with Demeter.

p. 233 Reading Check: Students should circle "You have no flowers here."

p. 233 Reading Strategy: Students may predict that she will have to spend some time in the underworld because of eating the seeds.

p. 233 Stop to Reflect: Sample answer: It's not fair that Persephone has to stay in the underworld just because Pluto grabs her and takes her there. She shouldn't have to be his wife.

p. 233 Literary Analysis: This myth explains why there are seasons.

p. 233 Reader's Response: Students' answers should indicate a knowledge of the story, of mythological gods and goddesses, and, perhaps, of compassion and fairness.

p. 233 Thinking About the Skill: Taking the time to predict what might happen next makes you think more deeply about the story. You think about the characters' actions so far to determine what they might do next or think about what kind of story it is (myth, legend, short story) to know how characters are likely to act.

"Icarus and Daedalus" by Josephine Peabody

p. 235 Activate Prior Knowledge: Students' descriptions should show an understanding that people often think that their abilities exceed what they can really do.

p. 235 Literary Analysis: Students should circle the words "cunning" and "cunningly."

p. 235 Reading Strategy: Students might predict Daedalus's plan to fly based on the hint that Daedalus was watching seagulls.

p. 235 Stop to Reflect: Sample answer: No, the plan wouldn't have worked. Based on modern knowledge, it takes more than feathers and flapping to fly. (However, what Daedalus says about riding air currents is correct-up to a point because a person would eventually fall.) Also, the atmosphere becomes colder, not hotter, the higher you get, so the wax would not have melted.

p. 236 Reading Strategy: Students might predict that Icarus will fall into the water.

The hint is that his father put wax on the wings and warned him not to fly too high.

p. 236 Literary Analysis: 1) He goes to the temple of Apollo in grief and hangs up the wings as an offering. 2) He has learned not to have too much pride in his abilities.

p. 236 Reader's Response: Students' answers should indicate an understanding of the story and the normal human feeling of wanting freedom.

Answers to Part 2

Burning Out at Nine?

p. 239 Read Magazine Articles: Students should underline three of the following: "He wakes up at 6 every weekday morning," "downs a five minute breakfast," "reports to school at 7:50," "returns home at 3:15," "hits the books from 5 to 9," and "goes to sleep at 10:30."

p. 239 Reading Strategy: The author thinks that children's schedules are too busy. Students should circle "Remember when enjoying life seemed like the point of childhood? Huh!"

p. 240 Reading Magazine Articles: Most students will agree that the information is not up-to-date because it was written in 1998.

p. 240 Reading Strategy: The use of experts' opinions strengthens the author's argument by giving the impression that what the author says is true.

p. 240 Reading Check: The average child spends 12 hours a week in unstructured play.

p. 241 Reading Informational Materials: The story does not mention the opinions of experts or parents who think that children today have enough leisure time. It also doesn't mention the opinions of those who think that children have too much leisure time.

Golden Girls

p. 243 Reading Strategy: Students may underline any of the following: "the lumps in their throats," "the chills that ran down their spines," "the eye-dampening sight," "high-stepping," "a steadily building roar of oh-oh-ooOOHH!" and the quote by A. J. Mleczko. These words suggest that the author is happy about the victory and can relate to the team's feelings of excitement and emotion.

p. 243 Reading Check: Sandra Whyte scored the last goal.

p. 244 Reading Strategy: Students should circle "(b) admiring." An example that supports the attitude might be the author's description of the "saves, many of them spectacular."

p. 244 Reading Check: Students should circle the word "grousing"; students should underline the word "gushing."

p. 244 Reading Informational Materials: The quotations support the author's attitude and also add interest because they contain the exact words of real people.

Memos

p. 246 Reading Strategy: You can locate the subject under "RE:" The subject is photo identification cards.

p. 246 Reading Check: Students should circle "On January 4th and 5th from 3pm to 5pm." Students should underline "All the new employees, anyone who is missing their picture on their employee identification badge."

p. 246 Reading Informational Materials: The headings come first. The first paragraph contains the most important information. Other details follow. The paragraphs are set up in block style. Each paragraph discusses one thing in direct language. The format works well because the information can be read quickly by employees, and they will know exactly what to do.

A Colony in the Sky

p. 248 Reading Magazine Articles: The topic is the colonization of Mars.

p. 248 Reading Check:
1. The more we know about the solar system's other planets, the better we will understand Earth.
2. This will make us safer.

p. 249 Reading Check:
Students may choose three of the following: general size, presence of water, length of days, or range of temperatures.

p. 249 Reading Strategy: Students should circle the word "recipe."

p. 249 Reading Strategy: Students may name two of the following: growing a garden, creating a wilderness, building a cathedral, or flying seeds over an ocean to drop them on a new island.

p. 250 Stop to Reflect: Students may say that terraforming Mars is a good idea because it will help us learn more about Earth. Others may say it is not a good idea because it is not possible. Answers will vary, but they should include valid reasons.

p. 250 Reading Informational Materials
Possible responses:
1. *Discover*
2. *National Geographic*
3. a science magazine
4. a magazine for school children

Algal Blooms

p. 252 Reading Textbooks: Possible response: It is helpful to include a picture because readers may not know what an algal bloom is or what it looks like.

p. 252 Reading Check: They found toxins.

p. 253 Reading Textbooks: Students should underline "the algae that grow rapidly . . . turn the color of the water red."

p. 253 Reading Strategy: Possible response: When there is an increase in the amount of nutrients in the water, red tides will occur more frequently.

p. 253 Reading Strategy: People may become seriously ill.

p. 254 Reading Textbooks: Possible response: If you didn't know the answer to the Checkpoint question, you could go back and reread the selection in order to find the answer.

p. 254 Reading Informational Materials: The feature is the heading "Integrating Technology." This heading helps readers locate specific information quickly.

How Do Rainmakers Make It Rain?

p. 256 Reading Essays: Possible response: A question can indicate a cause-and-effect relationship. The question in the title of this essay shows that the essay will explore the causes of rain.

p. 256 Stop to Reflect: Possible response: Making rain would be extremely valuable for land affected by drought. Rain could reduce the danger of fire in forests and would allow farmers to grow healthy crops in agricultural regions vulnerable to drought.

p. 257 Reading Check: The effect is that pure water in supercooled clouds does not freeze even when its temperature is below the freezing point. Students should circle the phrase "But the water can be 10 or 20 degrees below freezing (supercooled) without actually freezing."

p. 257 Reading Strategy:
1. 70 mm guns fire silver iodide particles at supercooled clouds.
2. Explosions spread the silver iodide particles at the right height.
3. Silver iodide helps water particles freeze and grow large.
4. When the particles become heavy enough, they fall to the ground as rain.

p. 257 Reading Informational Materials: The clouds must be supercooled in order to produce increased rainfall.

Signs

p. 259 Reading Signs: The most important information is the name of The National Oregon Trail Center. It is in the biggest and boldest type.

p. 259 Reading Check: Students should circle "5:00 PM."

p. 259 Reading Strategy: Your purpose might be to find out about special group times and rates. The sign tells you whom to call to get the information you need.

p. 260 Reading Strategy: A hiker might want to know what happened at the site.

p. 259 Stop to Reflect: Possible answer: You might find a historical sign at a museum or a historic landmark.

p. 259 Reading Informational Materials: First sign
1. hours of operation
2. cost to visit
3. who to contact to set up school trips
Second sign
1. what happened at the site
2. who is buried there

The Eternal Frontier

p. 262 Reading Essays: The author asks, "Where is the frontier now?" The author will support his position that the frontier lies in outer space.

p. 262 Reading Strategy: Possible response: By citing statistics and numerical facts, L'Amour supports his position that the new frontier is outer space. He cites statistics to show that the earth is overpopulated and overdeveloped, supporting his position that space exploration is a good idea.

p. 263 Reading Strategy: Possible response: The author's main purpose is to convince readers of the need to explore outer space. Students may underline any of the following: "Mankind is not bound by its atmospheric envelope . . . by any limits at all," "It is our destiny to move out . . . to dare the unknown," "It is our destiny to

achieve," "Yet we must not forget . . . did not exist before," or "The computer age has arisen . . . of computing devices."

p. 263 Reading Informational Materials: Possible response: This statement helps readers see L'Amour's point of view: If we do not explore new technologies and advances, we will never move forward or realize our full potential as a society.

Walking for Exercise and Pleasure

p. 265 Reading Government Publications: Headings break up the text into more manageable sections; they give clues about the information in each section so that readers can quickly find what they are looking for.

p. 265 Reading Check: Students should circle "39.5%." This number represents the group of people that had the highest percentage of regular walkers: men 65 years of age or older.

p. 265 Stop to Reflect: Possible responses: People walk for pleasure, to relieve tension, for exercise, to get somewhere, or to be alone. Students may say that their parents or grandparents walk. They should give reasons.

p. 266 Reading Strategy:
Students should choose four of the following:
1. Walking can improve the body's ability to consume oxygen.
2. It lowers a person's resting heart rate.
3. It reduces blood pressure.
4. It increases the efficiency of the heart and lungs.
5. It burns calories.

p. 265 Reading Check: Walking and running burn approximately the same amount of calories per mile. Running burns calories faster. Students should circle "Briskly walking one mile in 15 minutes burns just about the same number of calories as jogging an equal distance in 8 1/2 minutes."

p. 266 Reading Check:
1. It doesn't cost anything.
2. You can do it almost anytime and anywhere.
3. Almost anyone can do it.

p. 266 Reading Strategy: They are causes because they explain why walking is so popular.

p. 266 Reading Informational Materials: Students might point out the headings within the document, the bulleted list, the short paragraphs, or the clear, direct language.

The Iceman

p. 269 Reading Primary Research: Lessem's main point is to describe Ötzi, the frozen man, and the objects found with him. Lessem explains that these objects show what Ötzi's life and times were like.

p. 269 Reading Check: Students should circle "Ötzi may have been a shepherd . . . in search of messages from gods."

p. 270 Reading Check: Students should circle "hard flints" and "fine ax."

p. 270 Reading Strategy: Possible response: The bow and arrow found with Ötzi indicate that he was an experienced hunter. Based on the fact that there was a forest on the other side of the mountain, it is possible that Ötzi had planned to go hunting.

p. 271 Reading Primary Research: Students should note that the author bases his conclusion on the discovery of the flint and felt strips.

p. 271 Reading Strategy: Possible response: Ötzi died from the cold and snow. It took 5,000 years for his body to be discovered. Ötzi's belongings help people to better understand life during the Copper Age.

p. 271 Reading Informational Materials: Most students will probably agree that presenting evidence in the form of a story is very useful. It helps to put the evidence into context so that readers have a better understanding of the facts.

Let the Reader Beware

p. 276 Reading Guidelines: The title "Let the Reader Beware" refers to information on the Internet. The author is saying that information on the Internet frequently lacks credibility.

p. 276 Reading Strategy: The heading is a summary of the main idea of the paragraphs below it. Each heading is a tip for evaluating information on the Internet.

p. 277 Stop to Reflect: Students should indicate that the second meaning of *home page* is appropriate because the text refers to biographical information.

p. 277 Reading Guidelines: Students should underline sentences that include the following phrases: "current information is usually more valid and useful than older material" and "check out some of its links."

p. 278 Reading Check: Students should circle the sentence "Ideally, you should confirm the information with at least two other sources." It is especially important to triangulate data if it runs counter to your understanding or if you are using the information for an important decision.

p. 278 Reading Informational Materials: It is useful to have boxes in guidelines in order to call readers' attention to information that is particularly useful.

The Bill of Rights

p. 280 Reading Public Documents: Possible response: A document written today would be typed, not handwritten. It would be on regular white paper, not parchment paper.

p. 280 Reading Check: The Bill of Rights contains the first ten amendments to the Constitution.

p. 281 Reading Strategy: Check students' definitions of words.

p. 281 Reading Check: Possible response: The accused has the right to a speedy trial with an impartial jury. The accused also has the right to be informed of his or her crime and to be represented by a lawyer.

p. 282 Reading Informational Materials: Direct wording leaves less room for misinterpretation or misunderstanding of the laws.

Pandas

p. 284 Reading Research Reports: The main idea of this report is that the giant panda is a rare and special animal.

p. 284 Reading Check: Students should circle "the World Wildlife Fund (WWF)."

p. 285 Reading Strategy: Possible response: To what other animals are pandas related? Which zoos have pandas? How can I help the pandas?

p. 285 Stop to Reflect: Possible response:
1. Giant pandas can only live in cool bamboo forests.
2. Pandas do not have many babies.

p. 286 Reading Check: Possible response: Main Idea: The Chinese people and international conservation organizations are working hard to protect pandas. Supporting Detail: There are currently thirteen special panda reserves where some 800 pandas are living in safety.

p. 286 Reading Informational Materials: Authors use more than one source to get as much support for their ideas as they can and to provide varied information.

A Christmas Carol

p. 288 Reading Literary Criticism: The criticism is written for television viewers. The subtitle "Picks & Pans: Television" indicates that it is written for television viewers.

p. 288 Reading Strategy: Students should underline "But TNT's *Carol* would be worth watching if only for the lead performance of Patrick Stewart."

p. 288 Reading Strategy: The statement "Old story well told" indicates a positive response.

p. 289 Reading Literary Criticism: Possible responses: Popular actors attract audiences, so readers who recognize a favorite actor's name might watch the presentation simply to see that actor perform. The list also helps viewers to identify the characters and actors in the production.

p. 289 Reading Strategy: Students should underline "Handsome, wholesome, and finely tuned, the cable web's take on Charles Dickens's 1843 masterwork is TV at its classiest." Like the critic of the *People Weekly* review, the *Variety* critic praises the performance of the actors and the overall production.

p. 290 Reading Strategy: Students may underline any two of the following details: "there are many nifty strokes here that elevate the story above most interpretations," "peppered with sharp special effects that

don't encumber the narrative, this one gets it right," and "wonderful set pieces."

p. 290 Stop to Reflect: Some students will say the summary is detailed enough for an understanding of the review because the nature of a review is to summarize. However, others may say the summary does not give them enough information, and words such as "Scrooge's hum gets de-bugged" are vague and confusing.

p. 291 Reading Literary Criticism: Students should circle "The supporting actors are also first-rate."

p. 291 Reading Strategy: The critic says the strongest aspect of the performance is its "overall execution." The critic also says that Robert Halmi Sr.'s visuals are "the best so far" and that "the restrained magic is very effective."

p. 292 Reading Check: Students should circle *The Oakland Press*.

p. 292 Stop to Reflect Students should circle the letter *b*.

p. 292 Reading Strategy: He says the set design is "enormous and gorgeous."

p. 293 Stop to Reflect: Possible response: The actors the reviewer mentions by name are the "standouts," or leading performers.

p. 293 Reading Strategy: Students should underline any two of the following: "debut," "in perfect keeping with Wicks's toned-down production," "not quite as charismatic a miser as Coleman," "a much darker, even scarier Scrooge," and "that much more affecting."

p. 293 Reading Informational Materials: Possible response: Such literary criticisms might be found in magazines, newspapers, books, entertainment journals, and Web sites.

Making Fantasy Real

p. 295 Reading Responses to Literature: The birth and death dates might be included to provide background information about the author and to provide the context of the historical period during which the author lived.

p. 295 Reading Check: Students should circle two of the following: "Little Claus and Big Claus," "The Princess and the Pea," and "The Emperor's New Clothes."

p. 296 Reading Strategy: The writer says that in spite of the physical agony of the mermaid, the reader still feels that the prince is worth dying for.

p. 296 Reading Response to Literature: Possible response: You learn that Anderson believed that there is beauty in all creatures. The writer makes a connection between Anderson's own life and that of the swan in "The Ugly Duckling."

p. 296 Reading Informational Materials: Possible response: Some students may say that reading a response first is helpful because it provides background and context for the literary work. Others may say that a response might give away plot details and therefore spoil the fun of reading a literary work.

How to Use Your New Alarm Chronograph Timer

p. 298 Reading Directions: Studying a diagram is useful because it helps people familiarize themselves with the parts of a device before they learn how to operate it.

p. 298 Stop to Reflect: The list of features tells what functions the device is able to perform. In this case, the list of features tells you that you can use the watch to set an alarm or to time an event.

p. 298 Reading Strategy: Possible response: To begin any operation—whether setting the time or using the stopwatch—you need to be able to switch to the appropriate function, or mode.

p. 299 Reading Check: Students should circle the line "Turn to set function to ALARM."

p. 299 Reading Strategy Possible response: The best way to explain would be to demonstrate each of the steps for setting the alarm, and then to have the person set the alarm himself or herself.

p. 299 Reading Check: You could look in the list of features. Students should underline "Zero Match" in the list of features on p. 298.

p. 300 Reading Informational Materials: You would use the boldface headings to skip to the section with the directions for the countdown timer.

Bat Attacks?

p. 302 Reading Strategy: The main point of comparison is between wooden bats and aluminum bats.

p. 302 Reading Check: Some energy is lost when the ball compresses against the bat. The resulting friction releases energy as heat.

p. 302 Reading Strategy: Students should underline all sentences in the paragraph except the final sentence. The author's main point is that baseball players using aluminum bats hit balls farther than players using wooden bats.

p. 303 Stop to Reflect: The likely effect of professional players using aluminum bats would be more home runs. Some students might feel that more home runs would make baseball games more exciting by driving up scores. Others might feel that making home runs more common would detract from the special qualities of home runs and home run hitters.

p. 303 Reading Informational Materials: The author returns to his point that the use of aluminum bats could lead to an increase in injuries.

Tenochtitlan: Inside the Aztec Capital

p. 305 Reading Strategy: Possible response: Heads break up the text and help you find information on specific topics. The words in a head describe what that section is about.

p. 305 Stop to Reflect: Students might say the city map is similar to modern maps because it shows streets and waterways. They might also note that the city map is different because it lacks street names and because it shows buildings and other physical qualities of the city.

p. 305 Reading Check: Students should circle two of the following: "They built three causeways . . . to link the city with the mainland," "These were raised roads . . . supported on wooden pillars," "Parts of the causeways were bridges," "These bridges . . . prevented enemies from getting to the city," or "Fresh water was brought . . . along stone aqueducts."

p. 306 Stop to Reflect: Possible response: Tenochtitlan was a large city of one-story stone houses with flat roofs. It contained two temples on one side of the center square and the king's palace on the other side. The city was surrounded by water.

p. 306 Reading Social Studies Articles: Possible response: The Aztecs depended on corn and worshiped many gods and goddesses who were in charge of corn.

p. 307 Stop to Reflect: Possible response: The Aztecs were proficient stoneworkers and efficient architects.

p. 307 Reading Strategy: Students should underline "they think it may have been between one third . . . of the population," "The rest were nobility, craftspeople, and others," "Each chinampa . . . food for one family," "Most people . . . depended on food from outside the city."

p. 307 Reading Check: They got their food from farms outside the city.

p. 308 Reading Strategy: 1. The rich lived in stone houses in the center of the city. The houses were washed and shone white. They were large and surrounded by courtyards that were planted with flower and vegetable gardens. 2. The poor lived on the chinampas in wattle-and-daub houses. They lived with their families in small one- or two-room huts that were part of a compound. The poor also kept turkeys in pens and beehives for honey.

p. 308 Reading Informational Materials: Most students will probably agree that this article focuses on all of the key aspects of a social studies article. The article gives information about the geographic make up of the city, life inside the city, the customs and beliefs of the people, and the structure of the family.

Moving Mountains

p. 310 Reading Strategy: Students should circle the word "erosion." Students should underline "The Himalayas are gradually losing mass" and "the loss of mass is affecting the Himalayas' position on Earth's surface."

p. 310 Reading Check: The Himalayas are the highest mountains in the world.

p. 310 Reading How-to Essays: A list of the materials needed for the demonstration begins under the boldface head.

p. 311 Reading How-to Essays: Possible response: The numbering makes clear which step comes first and helps readers to focus on what to do in the correct order.

p. 311 Reading Informational Materials: After completing the experiment, readers have the information they need to understand the effects of erosion.

Answers to Part 1
Unit 1

The Cat Who Thought She Was a Dog and the Dog Who Thought He Was a Cat

p. 6 Reading Strategy: Students should circle *poor farmer.*

p. 6 Stop to Reflect: They may be poor but they still are generous.

p. 6 Reading Strategy: Students should circle *traveled from door to door, buying and selling things.*

peddler: someone who travels door to door, buying and selling things

p. 7 Reading Check: Students should circle *they saw problems they had never noticed before.*

p. 7 Stop to Reflect: Most students are likely to find the characters' behavior believable, since people are often dissatisfied with their appearance. Students may also mention people's common habit of staring in a mirror or complaining about something they don't like in their face.

p. 7 Reading Check: Students should write numbers near *first, the second,* and *third.* The first daughter pinched her nose; the second daughter pushed her chin; and the third daughter scrutinized her freckles.

p. 8 Read Fluently: After reading the sentence aloud, students should circle *deeply felt its poverty* and *envied the rich.*

p. 8 Literary Analysis: Possible response: The beauties of nature are more important than your own appearance; the world is more important than you.

p. 8 Literary Analysis: Possible response: A person's actions toward others are more important than his or her appearance; being kind and generous is more important than how you look.

Review and Assess

1. Possible response: poor, happy, loving

2. Marianna Skiba—missing tooth; first daughter—nose too snub and broad; second daughter—chin too narrow and long; third daughter—freckles; Kot—realizes she is not a dog.

3. Jan gives back the mirror because it has disrupted the house, and he realizes it is not good to spend so much time looking at one's self.

4. The following words help readers understand the meaning of the word *trinket:* jewelry and kerchiefs.

5. *glimpse:* a quick look

6. Students should check the first, fourth, and fifth sentences.

Two Kinds

p. 13 Reading Check: Students should circle *anything you wanted to be, rich,* and *instantly famous.*

p. 13 Reading Strategy: Students should circle *super, talent,* and *ed.* Possible completed sentence: A *supertalented* child is a child with more than normal talent.

p. 14 Stop to Reflect: Both are young girls of Chinese background.

p. 14 Reading Check: Students should circle *I felt as though I had been sent to hell. I whined and then kicked my foot a little when I couldn't stand it anymore.*

p. 14 Literary Analysis: Students should circle *Only ask you be your best. For your sake.*

p. 14 Read Fluently: Students should circle *He was deaf.*

p. 15 Reading Strategy: Students should circle *un* and *able.*

un-: not ; *-able:* able

p. 15 Reading Check: Students should circle *some nonsense that sounded like a cat running up and down on top of garbage cans.* Mr. Chong praises her because he is deaf.

p. 15 Stop to Reflect: No, Auntie Lindo does not think Jing-mei's mother is lucky. Auntie Lindo is really indirectly bragging that her daughter Waverly is more talented than Jing-mei.

p. 15 Literary Analysis: The correct answer is *C*; students should circle *bragged*

p. 16 Stop to Reflect: Students should predict that Jing-mei will play badly, since she has been taught by someone who does not hear her mistakes and praises playing that does not really sound good.

p. 16 Literary Analysis: Students should circle *jealousy*

p. 17 Stop to Reflect: Possible responses: yes; she has been prevented from being her true self and forced to do what she has no natural inclination or talent for; no, she is exaggerating her feelings because she is angry and ashamed and no longer wants to study the piano and resents being forced to do so.

p. 17 Reading Check: Students should circle and number (1) *those who are obedient* and (2) *those who follow their own mind.*

p. 17 Literary Analysis: Students should circle *I wanted to see it spill over.* They should also circle *anger.*

p. 18 Reading Check: Students should number four things that Jing-mei does that disappoint her mother: (1) She does not get straight A's or (2) become class president. (3) She does not get accepted to Stanford University. (4) She even drops out of college.

p. 18 Reading Strategy: Students should put a line between *forgive* and *ness.* Possible meaning: the act or state of forgiving

p. 18 Reading Check: The correct answer is *B.* Students should circle all or part of *I realized they were two halves of the same song.*

Review and Assess

1. Students should circle *famous* and *herself.*
2. Kind 1: those who are obedient
   Kind 2: those who follow their own mind

3. She is both an obedient daughter who wants love and approval and an independent daughter who has gone her own way.
4. *unlike:* not similar to
   childish: like a young person
   childhood: state or condition of acting like a young person
5. Possible motives for pushing Jing-mei to be famous: hope, pride, love
   Possible motives for arranging the talent show: pride, competitive spirit
   Possible motives for offering the piano: love, forgiveness
   Possible motives for agreeing to take piano lessons: desire for attention, respect for mother, need to please mother, need to gain approval
   Possible motives for refusing to take more lessons: shame, fear, need for independence
   Possible motives for saying hurtful words: anger, shame, desire to win the battle and end the piano lessons

My Furthest-Back Person (The Inspiration for *Roots*)

p. 23 Reading Check: Students should circle *slave forbears.*

p. 23 Reading Strategy: Students might put a line after the first comma, the second comma, *astonishment,* the colon, the second *Murray, well,* and *heard.* Accept reasonable variations: for example, some students may not put a line after *heard.* Students should circle C, Haley's great-grandparents

p. 24 Literary Analysis: Students should circle *wasn't, hadn't,* and *didn't.* Accept reasonable alternatives.

The use of italics adds to the conversational style by showing that *didn't* should be stressed, as it might be in a conversation. Also, it may call attention to the fact that Haley is knowingly breaking a grammatical rule by introducing a double negative.

p. 24 Reading Strategy: Students might put a line after *bent, herself,* and *overjoyed.* Accept reasonable variations; for example, some students may also put a line after *wrinkled.* Students should circle *she was so overjoyed.*

p. 24 Stop to Reflect: ko; She says *ko* means *banjo*. Students should circle *true*.

p. 25 Read Fluently: Students should say *Kamby* with the same /a/ sound that they use for the first /a/ in *Gambia*. Most students will circle *yes*.

p. 25 Stop to Reflect: The correct answer is *D*; he said he has to get to the Gambia River, and the paragraph before said the Gambia River flows near the old kingdom of Mali in Africa.

p. 25 Reading Strategy: Students might put a line after *something, fantasized* (or after the dash), *country*, the first comma, and the second comma. Accept reasonable variations.

Students should circle *very old men* and *who could tell centuries of the histories of certain very old family clans*. Accept reasonable variations.

A *griot* is a very old African man who can tell centuries of the histories of certain very old African family clans.

p. 26 Reading Check: the correct answer is *B*. Students might circle three or more of the following: *upriver, bank, ashore, (on) foot*.

p. 26 Reading Check: Students should circle *years*; Kunta Kinte was about 16 years old.

p. 26 Literary Analysis: In the text, students might circle *sob, bawling,* and *weeping*.

In the margin, students should circle *joy*. Haley is proud to have made this journey and made a critical connection to his own history.

p. 27 Stop to Reflect: Students should write *Annapolis*.

p. 28 Stop to Reflect: 42 out of 140; It shows that conditions were *foul*, as Haley says, and that the slaves were treated terribly.

p. 28 Literary Analysis: Students should circle *cargo, choice,* and *healthy*. Also accept *Gambia, Africa,* and/or *slaves* if students can explain these answers adequately.

Review and Assess

1. Kunta Kinte was an African who was the first person in Alex Haley's family to come to America.

2. He was kidnapped near the Gambia River, shipped to Annapolis, Maryland, and sold into slavery.

3. Students should include at least five details of information.

details of grandmother's story (African said his name was *Kin-tay*, banjo was *ko*, river was *Kamby Bolong; Kin-tay* chopping wood for a drum when kidnapped)—Cousin Georgia—Kansas City, Kansas

language sounds like Mandinka; *ko* is *kora*, an old African stringed instrument; *Kamby Bolong* is likely Gambia River—Dr. Jan Vansina—Wisconsin

Kin-tay is pronunciation of *Kinte*, clan name going back to old kingdom of Mali—Dr. Philip Curtin—Wisconsin (on phone to Dr. Vansina)

Griots in back country tell Kinte family history; family villages of Kintes include Kinte-Kundah and Kinte-Kundah Janneh-Ya—Gambians in capital—Gambia (Africa)

Kinte clan began in Old Mali; one member, Kairaba Kunta Kinte, settled in Juffure in Gambia; his youngest son, Omoro, wed Binta Kebba; they had 4 sons; eldest, Kunta Kinte, disappeared soon after the king's soldiers came, when he was 16 and had gone to chop wood for a drum—Kebba Kanga Fofana (griot)—Juffure, Gambia

Col. O'Hare's Forces (British "king's soldiers") sent to James Fort in Gambia mid-1967—government records—Britain

Lord Ligonier under Capt. Thomas Davies sailed on the Sabbath, July 5, 1767, from Gambia River to Annapolis; cargo included 3265 elephants' teeth, 800 pounds of cotton, 32 oz. Gambian gold, 140 slaves—British shipping records—Britain

Lord Ligonier arrived in Annapolis Sept. 29, 1767; only 98 slaves survived—Annapolis Historical Society—Annapolis, Maryland

sale of slaves from Gambia River, Africa, announced—microfilm copy of *Maryland Gazette*, Oct. 1, 1767, p. 2—Annapolis, Maryland

4. Students might draw a line after *upriver*, the first comma, *ashore*, and the second comma. Accept reasonable alternatives; for example, students might include a comma after the first *village*.

The travelers left their boat in Albreda.

Juffure was the village where the *griot* lived.

5. Possible responses: They are about his own family. They prove his grandmother's stories, which fascinated him as a boy. They are a source of pride to him as an African American. They reflect the origins of so many African American families. They show the pain and suffering of slavery.

A Day's Wait

p. 33 Reading Check: Students should circle *He is pale, he was shivering, and he looked as though it ached to move.*

p. 33 Stop to Reflect: Students should circle *You better go back to bed* and *When he comes downstairs, the boy is dressed and sitting by the fire.* They may speculate that Schatz fails to obey because he is stubborn, does not want to be sick and refuses to admit that he is, and/or because he wants to show his father that he is strong and not some sort of weakling who takes to his bed as soon as he gets a cold.

p. 33 Reading Strategy: *instructions:* lists that build information step by step; directions

p. 34 Literary Analysis: Students might circle *dark circles under his eyes; lay still;* and *seems detached and listless.* Some students may divide the second circled item into two items and fail to circle one of the others, or circle three items all together.

p. 34 Stop to Reflect: Accept all reasonable responses. Possible response: The boy thinks he is going to die and tells his father he need not stay to witness the painful experience.

p. 34 Stop to Reflect: Some students may say that having an outdoorsman and sportsman for a father may make the boy want to be particularly brave and strong. Others may say that being familiar with hunting may make him more matter-of-fact about facing death.

p. 35 Reading Check: He doesn't want anyone else to catch his illness. Students should circle *must not get what he has.*

p. 35 Literary Analysis: Students should circle *he asks whether taking the medicine will do any good* and *he evidently isn't taking it easy.*
Accept all reasonable internal conflicts. Possible response: Schatz's inner struggle

seems to be between his desire to face his illness bravely and his fear and worry about what will happen to him.

p. 36 Reading Strategy: Students should circle *thermometers* and *kilometers*; heat or temperature.

p. 36 Literary Analysis: Students should circle *relaxed* and *slack.* They may say that Schatz cries easily because he is relieved.

Review and Assess

1. The correct answer is *C*.
2. Students' wordings will vary. On the thermometers used in France, no one can live with a temperature of 44 degrees. So when Schatz heard the doctor say that his temperature is 102 degrees, he thinks he is sure to die.
3. Possible response: loving, patient, sympathetic, rugged
4. Schatz is (A) scared and (B) worried, BUT he tries to be (C) brave and (D) unselfish. Students may reversse the order of *A* and *B* and/or the order of *C* and *D*.
   Possible examples of (A) and (B): Schatz is pale; there are dark circles under his eyes; he is very stiff and tense; he seems detached and has trouble paying attention to his father's reading; he is evidently holding tightly onto his emotions; the next day he cries.
   Possible examples of (C) and (D): Schatz does not express his fears and holds tightly onto his emotions; he says he'd rather stay awake (i.e., to face death); even though it would be a comfort to have someone with him at this scary time, he tells father to leave because he knows it might bother the father to see his son die and orders people out of the room so that they don't catch the illness.
5. *evidently:* easily seen; clearly
   prescribed: ordered in writing; written in advance
   detached: unconnected

Was Tarzan a Three Bandage Man?

p. 41 Reading Strategy: The correct answer is *A*. Students might circle some or all of the following: *pigeon-toed walker, walked pigeon-toed,* and *a painful form of . . .*

p. 41 Literary Analysis: Students should circle: *"This is Jackie Robinson's walk,"* and *"He'd be faster if he didn't walk like that."* Students may find humor in the visual image of young Bill Cosby trying to walk pigeon-toed like Jackie Robinson or in the childish idea that imitating an admired athlete's style of walk would somehow reflect favorably on the person doing the imitating.

p. 42 Reading Strategy: *emulate:* to admire and imitate
Students might circle [Bill and his friends] *wear a Band-Aid* and/or *the Band-Aid is just for show. . . .*

p. 42 Read Fluently: Students should circle *sarcastic.*

p. 42 Stop to Reflect: The correct answer is *C.*

p. 43 Stop to Reflect: Washington was a famous African American teacher, and the mother wants her son to concentrate more on his education and less on sports and neighborhood antics.

p. 43 Reading Check: b. She will tell the father, and he will need not a mere bandage but stitches for his wounds.

p. 43 Literary Analysis: Students should circle *Our hero worshipping was backwards.*

Review and Assess

1. Possible response: Bill and his friends admire the sports stars and want to be like them. Imitating the sports stars is a fad of sorts and is considered "tough" and "cool" among the boys' peers.

2. T: The mother thinks Bill's behavior is silly.
   F: The mother is a friend of Jackie Robinson's mother.
   F: The mother thinks Bill's feet will fall off.
   T: The mother has a good sense of humor.
   F: The mother knows the names of all the popular sports heroes.

3. Suggested responses: Wearing the bandages does not really make anyone good at fighting. He is confusing the boys imitating the boxers with the actual boxers. He is confusing looking tough with being tough.

4. Suggested responses: Was the movie hero Tarzan tough and cool? Is the movie hero Tarzan worthy of imitation too?

5. Students should circle a *skin condition.*

6. *Purpose: to tell a funny, interesting story;* Possible examples: the boys imitating Jackie Robinson's pigeon-toed walk; the mother's remark, "He'd be faster if he didn't walk like that"; Bill imitating Buddy Helm's bowlegged walk; the boys wearing bandages to look like boxers; and so on.
   Purpose: to describe something important to him; Possible examples: Cosby indicating these athletes were "shining heroes" to him as a boy; showcasing his mother's wit or sense of humor; talking about what he did with his close friends of childhood (Fat Albert and the others).
   Purpose: to make a point about life or people's behavior; Possible examples: "Then, atheletes were sports stars even before they started to incorporate themselves"; "Our hero worshipping was backwards."

Unit 2

In Search of Our Mother's Gardens

p. 48 Stop to Reflect: No. She worked past sundown, raising and caring for her family.

p. 48 Reading Strategy: Students should circle *A.*

p. 48 Thinking Ahead: Students should circle *B.* Students might explain that all the other choices are famous, celebrated people. In contrast, a poor woman who made quilts might be considered low.

p. 49 Literary Analysis: No. Students should circle *our, mothers,* and *grandmothers.*

p. 49 Literary Analysis: Possible response: She sees that her mother has given Walker her manner or style in addition to her stories.

p. 50 Literary Analysis: The correct answer is *B.*

p. 50 Reading Check: The correct answer is *C.* Students should circle *magic, magnificent, creativity,* and *art.*

p. 51 Reading Strategy: The correct answer is *B. Intruded* means "interrupted." Students may say that the meaning of the root -*trud*- suggests that being intruded upon is like being pushed.

p. 51 Read Fluently: The correct answer is *D*.

p. 51 Reading Check: Students should circle *love of beauty* and *respect for strength*. The correct answer is *A*.

Review and Assess

1. She thinks they owe their creative spirit to the women who have lived before them.

2. Students should check *She and her husband worked hard . . .* and *No matter how plain their house. . . .*

3. The correct answer is *B*.

4. The correct answer is *D*.

5. Students may list: her mother's perseverance in planting a garden wherever she lived; her strength in caring for it; her ability to make it beautiful; and her ability to work hard for her family.

6. -*liter*-: *literate*/able to read; *literacy*/ability to read.

   -*nym*-: *synonyms*/words that mean the same thing; *antonyms*/words that have opposite meanings.

   -*magni*-; *magnify*/to enlarge; *magnificent*/large in beauty, wonder or power.

Seventh Grade

p. 56 Stop to Reflect: Most students will say it is easier to study their native language because they begin with a stronger foundation. However, some students may note that the grammar and vocabulary of even a native language may be complex to learn.

p. 56 Reading Check: The correct answer is *B*.

p. 56 Literary Analysis: The correct answer is *C*. Possible response: He makes it seem as though the boys don't really understand that the models are scowling as a pose, not as a way of life.

p. 57 Read Aloud: Possible response: Michael is Mexican but not good at Spanish; Victor is not good at Math. Victor is taking French.

p. 57 Think Ahead: Possible response: It is possible that everything he imagines will not happen. It may not be his "lucky year."

p. 57 Reading Strategy: Students may say *on the sly* means "sneakily." Students should circle *catch her eye*, on page 57. Catch her eye means "to get her attention by getting her to look at him."

p. 58 Literary Analysis: Possible response: Students may like Victor because he is trying his best, but is not able to be as smooth as he wants.

p. 58 Stop to Reflect: Possible response: No. The girls are probably staring because Michael looks strange.

p. 58 Literary Analysis: Students may circle *pretended to read*, or *stretched out lazily in an attempt to disguise his snooping*. Students may circle parts of these phrases that get at the gist of the idea.

p. 59 Reading Check: Possible response: They are not real words. Students should circle *to bluff his way out by making noises that sounded French.*

p. 60 Stop to Reflect: Teresa might be able to help Victor in Math. Possible response: They may become friends.

p. 60 Reading Check: The correct response is *D*. Students should circle *shame* and *love*.

p. 60 Stop to Reflect: Victor goes to the library to learn French ahead of his classmates and ahead of Teresa.

Review and Assess

1. Victor signs up for French because Teresa was taking French, too.

   Victor is slow to leave homeroom because Teresa was still there, talking to the teacher.

   Victor goes outside during lunch because he thinks Teresa is eating outside.

   Victor pretends to know French to impress Teresa.

   Victor gets French books at the library because he wants to learn French so Teresa won't discover he does not speak the language.

2. Possible responses: Victor is embarrassed when he tries scowling. Victor is embarrassed when he says "Teresa" is a noun. Victor is embarrassed when he pretends to speak French.

3. Possible responses: Seventh grade is a time of fun, anxiety, uncertainty, or of a blooming interest in girls/boys, or of feeling self-conscious.

4. Possible responses: Amused: the incident of scowling; the boy's language when he tries to speak French. Understanding; the French teacher is kind to Victor; some of Victor's embarrassed, self-conscious feelings.

5. *Making a face* means moving the features on your face to show an expression.
   Catch her eye means "to get her attention by getting her to look."

Melting Pot

p. 65 Literary Analysis: Students may circle *a close friend of my two boys.* This gives the essay an informal tone because it relates to the author's personal experiences.

p. 66 Reading Check: Students should circle and number these words: (1) the old-timers; (2) the moneyed-professionals; (3) the old immigrants; (4) the new ones.

p. 66 Stop to Reflect: Because she is "one of them."

p. 67 Literary Analysis: Possible response: She probably likes them. She describes their reaction as they watch the glass workers. She describes *sitting with them and watching neighborhood activities.*

p. 68 Literary Analysis: Students should mark *calamari* with A. Students should mark *sushi* with B. Students should mark *bait* with C.

p. 68 Reading Strategy: 1. described in a very general way; 2. a very tense place; 3. two things that don't mix easily.

Review and Assess

1. People who call America a melting pot mean that the country's values and traditions are generated by the mixing of many different groups. No one culture retains its values—instead a new set of values and traditions comes from the mixing of cultures.

2. Students should check *It is most like a melting pot when people deal with each other person-to-person.*

3. Students should identify these conflicts: old-timers vs. young professionals; old immigrants vs. new immigrants.

4. Anna Quindlen is a young professional because she has a career and small children. She is an old-timer because she has lived in the community for a long time. She is an old immigrant because her grandparents immigrated to America.

5. *Taking over* means "taking control."

6. Possible response: Personal experience: Quindlen describes what it was like when she moved on to the block eight years earlier.
   Personal feelings: Quindlen defends her neighborhood.
   Informal language: half a dozen elderly men; I like you.
   Humor: The antiques store used to be a butcher shop.

The Hummingbird that Lived Through Winter

p. 73 Stop to Reflect: Possible responses: Good point: They will feel comfortable among people who share customs and language. Bad point: They may not learn the new language or customs.

p. 73 Reading Check: In the text, students should circle *wild and wonderful, plants, bushes,* and *trees.* In the minor column, students should circle *birds, butterflies,* and *bees.*

p. 74 Read Fluently: Possible response: What color is the bird? Why does it shoot away? What does it eat?

p. 74 Literary Analysis: Students should circle *wonderful, suspended,* and *most alive.* Student should draw boxes around *helpless, pathetic,* and *heartbreaking.* The correct answer is *D.*

p. 75 Literary Analysis: Students may circle *signs of fresh life; the warmth of the room; the vapor . . . ;* or *the change.*

p. 75 Reading Strategy: Students should draw a line between *rest* and *less.* Restless means without resting, or without being able to rest.

p. 76 Think Ahead: Students may predict that he will live because he is shown such care.

p. 76 Stop to Reflect: Possible response: He means that people help all small animals, or that small animals need the protection of humans.

Review and Assess

1. Possible responses: 1. Dikran blows warm air on the bird. 2. He feeds it honey. 3. They let the bird go.

2. Possible response: Students may say that Dikran knows it is better for a bird to be free than for it to be house bound.

3. Students should place a check before the following statements: *He can barely see;*

He loves and respects nature; He respects the freedom of living things.

4. Students should place a check before the following statements. Each statement is followed by an appropriate explanation. *Hope or renewal/* He lives through winter. *The fragile or delicate nature of life:* The tiny bird could have died. The beauty and wonder of nature: *His recovery is amazing; the birds in spring are beautiful.*

5. Hummingbird: a bird that hums. Helpless: Without being able to help. Heartbreaking: Something that breaks a heart; something that is painfully sad.

Unit 3

The Third Wish

p. 81 Reading Strategy: (a) untangle. Students should circle *trying* and *entangled.*

p. 81 Literary Analysis: Students should circle the words *a little man all in green.* The creature was freed from its prison.

p. 81 Literary Analysis: Possible response: Mr. Peters expects three wishes because he knows the pattern of older fairy tales. Characters usually do not know what to expect.

p. 82 Reading Check: Students should circle *he was a little lonely* and *had no companion for his old age.*

p. 82 Literary Analysis: He gets his wish. He gets a wife almost instantly.

p. 83 Stop to Reflect: Possible response: She may really be a swan.

p. 83 Literary Analysis: (d) He knows what happens in fairy tales.

p. 84 Literary Analysis: Students should circle *drives in the car* and *listen to the radio.*

p. 84 Read Fluently: Possible response: Rhea is her swan-sister.

p. 84 Stop to Reflect: Possible response: Mr. Peters may wish that he is together with his wife after he dies because he loves her so much.

p. 85 Literary Analysis: Students should circle *no.* Students should circle the last sentence that describes Mr. Peters holding the withered leaf.

Review and Assess

1. He rescues a swan tangled in the weeds.

2. (b) He seems fed up with granting wishes and makes fun of human beings.

3. Possible response: His third wish was to be together in spirit with his wife. He knew she was still his companion.

4. Students should check *We are never comfortable . . . , Love sometimes means letting go . . . , What we wish for . . .* and *There are many different . . .*

5. In the first column students should list *three wishes; animals transforming;* and *unexpected outcomes.* In the second column students should list *a car; radio;* and *the offer of a trip around the world.*

6. The correct answers are *C* and *D.*

The Charge of the Light Brigade

p. 90 Literary Analysis: The correct answer is *A.*

p. 90 Read Fluently: The correct answer is *A.*

p. 90 Stop to Reflect: The correct answer is *D.*

p. 91 Reading Check: Students should answer *yes*. Students should circle *All that was left of them, Left of six hundred.*

Review and Assess

1. Students should check *They are riding . . . They are lightly armed . . . They are attacking.*
2. The correct answer is *A*.
3. Many of the soldiers are killed.
4. The correct answer is *B*.
5. On the first line students should write *cannon; them*. On the second line students should write *trapped*. On the third line students should write *battle*.
6. Fired on as frequently as rain drops in a storm.

The Californian's Tale

p. 96 Literary Analysis: Students should circle *prospecting, pick, pan, horn,* and *strike*.

p. 96 Reading Strategy: Students should circle the first sentence in the paragraph.

p. 97 Literary Analysis: People were invited in and made welcome. Students should circle the last sentence of the paragraph.

p. 97 Stop to Reflect: (c) He misses his own home.

p. 98 Reading Check: (a) educated and a good storyteller. Students should circle *people who know things, and can talk—people like you.*

p. 98 Read Fluently: Possible response: He may be lonely.

p. 99 Stop to Reflect: Student should write *No*. Possible response: He may be embarrassed.

p. 100 Reading Check: (b) thoughtful. Students should circle the entire paragraph to support their answer.

p. 100 Read Fluently: disbelief or concern.

p. 100 Literary Analysis: very; extremely.

p. 101 Literary Analysis: Students should circle *fiddle, banjo, clarinet (p. 100), rattling dance-music,* and *big boots*.

p. 101 Literary Analysis: Students should circle *right up the road.*

p. 101 Reading Strategy: (a) Henry lost his mind when he lost his wife, and he gets worse on the anniversary of that loss. His friends play along to try to help him get through it.

p. 102 Stop to Reflect: (d) all of the above

Review and Assess

1. (d) It is pretty and shows a woman's touch.
2. Students should write a *T* in front of *Henry talks about . . . , Henry lost his wife . . . , Henry's wife was well liked . . . ,* and *Henry's wife was an educated woman . . .* Students should write an *F* in front of *Henry's wife was an orphan* and *Henry's wife knew little about . . .*
3. The miners pretend she is coming home to help Henry through this rough time of the year.
4. (a) It could be lonely but those who were there were often kind and friendly.
5. First line: *friendly; folksy*. Second line: *colorful; descriptive*. Third line: *rural; homey*. Fourth line: *gathering together; playing musical instruments*.
6. Thirty-five years ago I panned for gold but I never found any.

Four Skinny Trees

p. 107 Reading Check: (a) thin and scrawny. Students should circle *skinny* and *pointy*.

p. 107 Literary Analysis: (b) If one person in a group loses his or her way, the whole group is affected.

p. 108 Reading Strategy: (c) alone in a difficult world

Review and Assess

1. Both the speaker and the trees are skinny.
2. The speaker and the trees grow up in a poor city neighborhood.
3. Students should put a check in front of *strength, hope,* and *pride*.
4. First sentence: Students might write *Children do not belong in ghettos but often are raised there.* Second sentence: Students might write *Individual strengths are often hidden.* Third sentence: Students might write *Inner strength helps us reach high goals.*
5. Students should circle *(a) roots* and *(b) the trees' branches*

Unit 4

The Night the Bed Fell

p. 113 Reading Check: Students should circle *it was wobbly and the heavy headboard would crash down on father's head in case the bed fell, and kill him.*

p. 113 Literary Analysis: Students should circle *He thinks he needs to wake up every hour. Otherwise he might suffocate to death.*

p. 114 Reading Strategy: Students should explain why they do or do not think it is significant.

p. 114 Reading Strategy: The correct answer is (c).

p. 114 Reading Check: Top Floor Attic: Mr. Thurber; Next Room: James and Briggs; In Hall: Rex, the dog; Across the Hall: Roy; Floor Below Attic: Mrs. Thurber and Herman

p. 115 Reading Strategy: Students should explain what they think might happen. Yes. It is a significant event. It starts the chain of events.

p. 115 Stop to Reflect: It's funny because the reason he uses the camphor is so that he can sniff it to revive his breathing because he is afraid he will stop breathing at night.

p. 115 Read Fluently: Students should circle (b).

p. 116 Literary Analysis: Students should circle the following: *He thinks the house is on fire; mother thinks he is trapped under his bed; "He's dying!" . . . "I'm all right!" Briggs yelled.*

p. 116 Reading Check: Students should circle the following: *Father caught a cold.*

p. 116 Stop to Reflect: Students should explain why they do or do not think it is funny.

Review and Assess

1. The correct answer is (a).
2. He does these things because he is afraid he will stop breathing at night.
3. Mother: She thinks her husband is trapped under the bed. Cousin Briggs:He thinks he is suffocating and everyone is trying to save him. Rex the Dog: He jumps on Briggs, thinking he is the culprit.

4. He probably exaggerated Briggs' fear of suffocation. The story of his Aunt Sarah leaving money for burglars outside her house might be an exaggeration. The story about his Aunt Gracie is probably an exaggeration when he says she piled shoes "about her house." The story of the dog jumping on Briggs might also be an exaggeration.

5. Students should check the following: The father goes up to the attic to sleep; Young James Thurber's cot collapses; The mother fears the attic bed fell and hurt or killed the father; Brother Herman yells to try to calm mother; Cousin Briggs pours camphor all over himself; Rex attacks Briggs; The father thinks the house is on fire and comes downstairs. Students should circle *Young James Thurber's cot collapses* as the event that causes all of the confusion.

All Summer in a Day

p. 121 Read Fluently: Students should circle (a).

p. 121 Literary Analysis: Students should circle the following: *Venus has known nothing but rain.*

p. 121 Reading Check: They're the children of the men and women who came to Venus from Earth to set up a space colony.

p. 122 Reading Check: Students should circle *nine.* They would have been two years old when they saw the sun before.

p. 122 Reading Strategy: Margot: quiet and shy; William: bold and mean

p. 122 Literary Analysis: Students should circle the following: *in the echoing tunnels of the underground city.*

p. 122 Stop to Reflect: Possible answer: She only sings songs about the sun because she misses the sun and dislikes the rain.

p. 123 Reading Strategy: Students should circle the following contrasts: *[Margot has] lived on Venus for only five years. Before that, she lived on Earth./The rest of the children have lived all of their lives on Venus. She remembers the sun./Because they were only two when they saw the sun,* *the don't remember it.* Possible answer: Margot's past experience might be considered a "crime" to the others because she is able to remember something they wish they could remember. They are probably jealous.

p. 123 Reading Strategy: Students should circle the following: *Margot's parents are thinking of moving back to earth.* The children probably hate her for this because they are jealous.

p. 123 Reading Check: Margot came to Venus five years ago, when she was four. She came from Earth.

p. 124 Reading Strategy: Students should circle the following words: *protesting, pleading,* and *crying.* The other children are mean.

p. 124 Stop to Reflect: Students should explain what they think will happen to Margot.

p. 124 Literary Analysis: Students should circle *the jungle burned with sunlight.* The correct answer is (b) thick rain forest.

p. 125 Reading Check: She cries because the raindrop means the sunlight is ending and the rain will start again soon.

p. 126 Stop to Reflect: Students will probably say that she will feel very angry and sad.

Review and Assess

1. For seven years, it has rained constantly.
2. she is from Earth and remembers the sun; are mean to her; regret.
3. The correct answer is (b).
4. Students should check the following: Children can be mean to one another; Outsiders are often treated badly; If you are mean, you may regret it later.
5. 1. "Sometimes there were light showers; sometimes there were heavy storms; but always there was rain." 2. "She doesn't play games with the other children in the echoing tunnels of their underground city." 3. "It was the color of flaming bronze and it was very large. And the sky around it was a blazing blue tile color."
6. *Similarities:* Margot and her classmates 1. live on Venus 2. are nine years old 3. are eager to see the sun

Differences: 1. Margot remembers the sun. Her classmates do not remember the sun. 2. She has been living on Venus for only five years. Her classmates have been living on Venus their entire lives. 3. Margot did not get to see the sun because she was locked away in a closet. Her classmates went out and played in the sun.

The Highwayman

p. 131 Reading Check: Students should write *night* on the line. Then, they should circle the following text: *The highways, or roads, had many inns where travelers stopped at night. Sometimes travelers were held up by robbers called highwaymen.*

p. 131 Stop to Reflect: Students should circle (a). The details that point to the answer are *a French cocked-hat, a bunch of lace at his chin, a coat of claret velvet, breeches of brown doeskin,* and *a jeweled twinkle.*

p. 132 Literary Analysis: He's probably jealous and dislikes the highwayman. He might try to get the highwayman in trouble.

p. 132 Reading Strategy: The highwayman has probably robbed someone.

p. 133 Literary Analysis: Students should circle the following: *they gag Bess and tie her to her bed by the window. They tie a gun called a musket to her, with the barrel below her heart.*

p. 133 Read Fluently: The correct answer is (c).

p. 134 Literary Analysis: The following words add to the suspense: *Nearer he came and nearer!; Her eyes grew wide for a moment; she drew one last deep breath.* Students might wonder if Bess will be able to let the highwayman know that the soldiers are after him.

p. 134 Literary Analysis: He wants to go back to fight the soldiers because of what they did to Bess. Students should circle the following: *he spurred like a madman; with white road smoking behind him and his rapier brandished high.*

p. 134 Reading Check: Bess shot herself while trying to sound off a gun shot to warn the highwayman that the soldiers were after him.

Review and Assess

1. He doesn't want anyone to see him because he is wanted by the law.

2. Highwayman: dashing, romantic, loyal; Bess: beautiful, romantic, brave, loyal; Tim: jealous.

3. The correct answer is (d).

4. The following details help build suspense: 1. Tied up and gagged, Bess desperately wants to warn her love of the danger that awaits him. 2. "The highwayman came riding/The redcoats looked to their priming." 3. "Nearer he came and nearer! Her face was like a light."

5. Tim probably told the authorities that the highwayman was at the inn because he likes Bess and is jealous of their love.

6. *Cause:* Bess pulls the trigger because she is trying to sound off a gun shot to warn the highwayman that the soldiers are waiting to get him. *Effects:* Bess kills herself. The highwayman hears the warning shot and rides away.

Amigo Brothers

p. 140 Think Ahead: Students should circle *each youngster had a dream of someday becoming lightweight champion of the world.* Problems can develop in their friendship if they someday have to compete for a title.

p. 140 Reading Check: What: division finals; When: seventh of August, two weeks away.

p. 140 Reading Strategy: The wall is probably created by the tension they feel because they have to compete against each other.

p. 141 Literary Analysis: Students should circle *Antonio nodded* and underline *Antonio.*

p. 141 Reading Check: No. Students should circle *only one of us can win.*

p. 141 Read Fluently: gotta: got to; don'tcha: don't you

p. 142 Literary Analysis: Felix: he had figured out how to psyche himself for tomorrow's fight; Antonio: Antonio was also thinking of the fight/Antonio went to sleep hearing the opening bell for the first round. The narrator is omniscient or "all knowing."

p. 142 Reading Strategy: Yes. His worry and concern over their friendship shows he cares.

p. 142 Stop to Reflect: Students should explain what they think the boys are thinking.

p. 143 Reading Strategy: The correct answer is (c). The words *He [Felix] missed a right cross as Antonio slipped the punch and countered with one-two-three lefts that snapped Felix's head back* help you make the inference.

p. 144 Literary Analysis: Felix: Felix's legs momentarily buckled; Antonio: his long legs turned to jelly. The author uses their first names, rather than just "he" to make the shift in point of view.

p. 145 Reading Check: Neither boy is winning.

p. 145 Stop to Reflect: They probably keep fighting because they've become completely wrapped up in what they are doing and they don't hear the bell.

p. 145 Reading Strategy: The correct answer is (d). Students should circle *No matter what the decision, they knew they would always be champions to each other.*

p. 145 Reading Check: The announcer points to no one as the winner because the boys have already left the ring, arm in arm.

Review and Assess

1. The correct answer is (b).

2. How it brings them together: they worked out together and went running together. How it drives them apart: They have to compete against each other, and only one person can win.

3. Tall—A; short—F; dark—F; fair—A; boxes better when he comes in close—F; boxes more gracefully—A; has better moves as a boxer—F; keeps boring in on his opponent—F

4. Friendship is more important than winning.

5. Felix: 1. Felix knew they could not "pull their punches," or hold back when they fought 2. he had figured out how to psyche himself
   Referee: The referee was stunned by their savagery.
   Crowd: The fear soon gave way . . .

6. Antonio and Felix work very hard to fulfill their dreams about boxing; The Golden Gloves is an important tournament in the world of boxing.

Unit 5

Our Finest Hour

p. 151 Reading Check: Students should circle the following words: *means sitting there in the studio and telling some stories into the camera and introducing the reports and pieces that other reporters do.* Students should circle (a) the main announcer.

p. 151 Literary Analysis: Some problems will probably arise. The people who are usually in charge are away.

p. 152 Reading Strategy: Students will probably circle the following text: *It was not the story I had introduced.* Students should circle answer (c).

p. 152 Literary Analysis: They thought they had fixed the problem, but they had not. A political story from Washington, D. C. was supposed to be introduced, but pictures of people in France pretending to be dead to show the dangers of smoking came up on the monitor.

p. 152 Stop to Reflect: Students should circle the following text: *since nobody in authority at CBS News, New York, had seen it or knew what was coming next, they decided to dump out of it.* Possible answer: People pretending to be dead might be disturbing to some people.

p. 153 Literary Analysis: Students should circle the following: *French people pretending to be dead and myself, bewilderment and all.* The fact that he sees himself is funny because he's feeling bewildered by what is happening, he doesn't realize they are coming back to him, and then he sees himself with a look of bewilderment on his face.

p. 153 Read Fluently: Students should circle (a).

Review and Assess

1. Students should circle answer (d).
2. Students should circle *calm* and *professional*.
3. No. His words are a follow-up to the fill-in producer yelling "What is going on?" so he was probably having fun with what had happened.
4. **Supposed to Happen:** He introduced his first report. **Actually Happened:** He saw himself on the monitor and then a different story was introduced. **Supposed to Happen:** He introduced a political story from Washington, D. C. **Actually Happened:** Pictures of people in France pretending to be dead to show the dangers of smoking came up on the monitor. **Supposed to Happen:** Osgood introduced a story about rafting. **Actually Happened:** Nothing happened on the monitor.
5. Any of the following details show that the author's purpose is mainly to entertain:
   - Osgood starts by explaining that he introduced his first report and then builds to make his point that a story came on that was not the story he introduced.
   - Then, Osgood explains that a political story from Washington, D.C. was supposed to be introduced, but pictures of people in France pretending to be dead to show the dangers of smoking came up on the monitor.
   - He explains how the monitor shows him with a bewildered look on his face.
   - He tells us how the fill-in producer screamed so loud "half of America" could hear him.
   - He ends his story by telling us the humorous way that the head of CBS responded to the incident.

Cat on the Go

p. 158 Literary Analysis: Students should circle the following: *I went home for a blanket and brought 'im round to you.*

p. 158 Reading Strategy: Students should circle answer (b). The words *terrible wound* show us that the cat is very badly hurt. The words *There's nothing anybody can do about . . . about that* also show us that it seems like a hopeless situation for the cat.

p. 159 Think Ahead: Some students may think he will survive because his purrs are a positive sign.

p. 159 Reading Strategy: Students should circle (a) try.

p. 159 Stop to Reflect: He needs to sit still so that he can rest and heal.

p. 159 Reading Check: The correct answer is (b).

p. 160 Literary Analysis: He is playful and friendly.

p. 160 Reading Check: Students should circle *odd* and *unusual*.

p. 160 Literary Analysis: Students should circle *seemed to enjoy himself, enjoyed the slides*, and *was very interested in the cakes*.

p. 161 Read Fluently: Students should circle *He's a natural mixer* and *cat-about-town*.

p. 161 Stop to Reflect: Students should explain why they think he is named Tiger. Students might mention that tigers are in the cat family. Others might mention that tigers are very strong.

p. 161 Literary Analysis: Possible answer: considerate and generous.

p. 162 Think Ahead: Possible response: He's probably visiting an event in the area.

p. 162 Literary Analysis: Students should circle *delight*. The correct answer is (a) She is warm and caring.

Review and Assess

1. The correct answer is *C*.

2. He purrs after being seriously injured. He likes to be a cat-about-town.

3. The Herriots are very sad about returning Oscar, but they also realize that he should be with his original owners because they had him first and they love him very much.

4. The correct answer is *B*.

5. Oscar the Cat: friendly and affectionate; James Herriot: skilled as a doctor and a good storyteller; Helen Herriot: caring

6. Oscar was always visiting people and places. Let's try this. The two boys screamed with excitement.

The Luckiest Time of All

p. 167 Reading Strategy: Students should circle the following text: *somethin like the circus.*

p. 167 Reading Check: Students should circle the following text: *wanted to join that thing and see the world.*

p. 167 Literary Analysis: Students should circle the following text: *cutest one thing in the world next to you.* It is an exaggeration because she doesn't really mean that it's the cutest in the world, she is just stressing the point that she thinks it is a very cute dog.

p. 168 Literary Analysis: Students should circle *I flew*. She probably exaggerates so that her great-granddaughter can appreciate the excitement of the moment.

p. 168 Stop to Reflect: The traits Elzie seems to like are kindness and gentleness. Students should circle the following: *he had picked up that poor dog to see if he was hurt, cradlin him and talking to him soft and sweet.*

p. 169 Read Fluently: Elzie says she is luckier than anybody for meeting her husband, but then in the last sentences she says that *most* of the time she thinks she's lucky. There are probably times when she's frustrated with her husband, so she's being funny when she says "Least mostly I think it."

Review and Assess

1. Students should circle two of the following words: adventurous, fun-loving, and shy. Adventurous: they want to join Silas Greene to see the world. Fun-loving: They want to join in on the excitement when they see the dancing dog and people throwing money for the dog. Shy: Elzie says she felt shy when she walked toward Amos.

2. Students should circle the following words: heroic, thoughtful, protective, nice.

3. It was unlucky because it hit the dog's nose and the dog chased her. It's lucky because the dog-chase led to her meeting her husband.

4. One example is when she calls the dog the "cutest one thing in the world next to you." Another example is when she refers to Amos as the "finest fast runnin hero in . . . Virginia." Another example is when she says the dog "lit out after me and I flew."

5. After all those years, she can look back and see how important that funny experience was in her life. She can realize how different life probably would have been for her if she had not had that experience. Certain moments probably stand out in her mind more than other

moments, so her use of hyperbole helps stress those particular moments and add more excitement to her story.

6. (c) spotted; (b) holding gently

How the Snake Got Poison

p. 174 Reading Check: Students should circle *ladder*. The ladder is probably supposed to lead to heaven.

p. 174 Read Fluently: Students should circle *Ah* for *I* and *de* for *the*.

p. 175 Literary Analysis: The snake feels he needs protection so he won't be stomped on and so that his generation won't be killed off, but the small animals feel they need protection from the snake so he won't kill them and their generations.

p. 175 Reading Strategy: Students should circle *B*. Students should explain why they agree or disagree.

p. 175 Stop to Reflect: If the snake sees his enemy he will probably go after him.

Review and Assess

1. God gives the snake poison so that he'll be protected and so that his generation won't be killed off.

2. The correct answer is *C*.

3. The story couldn't end that way because in reality snakes are poisonous and have rattles.

4. The small animals complain that the snake's poison is killing their generations. The snake explains that he has to protect himself because all he sees is feet coming to step on him and he can't tell who is his enemy and who is his friend.

5. Students should check the following: *A snake's rattles protect small animals from the snake; All types of animals created by God deserve to remain on earth; Animals have special traits or abilities to help them survive.*

Unit 6

Rikki-tikki-tavi

p. 180 Reading Check: Students should circle a *small furry animal that kills snakes*. The word *bungalow* is also explained in this paragraph. Students should put a box around the word *bungalow* and circle the words *one-story house*.

p. 180 Stop to Reflect: Students should circle *Here's a dead mongoose. Lets have a funeral.* It is funny because Rikki was not dead.

p. 180 Literary Analysis: (b) He is nosey. Students should circle *he is eaten up from the nose to tail with curiosity. The motto of all the mongoose family is "Run and find out.*

p. 181 Reading Check: Students should circle *One of our babies fell out of the nest yesterday and Nag ate him.*

p. 181 Reading Strategy: (b) they will fight. Students may write *The father says he will protect Teddy from snakes.*

p. 181 Literary Analysis: (b) rising action

p. 182 Reading Strategy: Rikki thinks he will fight Nag later.

p. 182 Reading Check: Students should circle *It must be the head.* Possible response: Yes, because Rikki is a born snake killer.

p. 183 Literary Analysis: Rikki will defeat Nag.

p. 183 Reading Strategy: (a) try to kill Nagaina. Even with Nag dead, Nagaina is still a danger.

p. 184 Stop to Reflect: Students should check *She is a concerned mother, She is angry . . . ,*

p. 184 Read Fluently: (a) He wants to take her attention away from the family.

p 185 Literary Analysis: Nagaina is killed by Rikki. Killing the last villain helps fix the problem.

p. 185 Literary Analysis: He has become a hero and is welcomed by the whole family.

Review and Assess

1. Students should circle *brave, nosey.*

2. Mongooses are born to kill snakes; Rikki wants to protect Teddy from the cobra.

3. (d) He wants to clear the garden of deadly cobras.

4. 1. Nag eats a baby bird. 2. Nagaina sneaking up behind Rikki to do him harm. 3. Karait striking at Rikki.

5. The climax is when Nag is killed.

6. Students should write *We learn that Rikki is a natural predator of snakes; Rikki hears Nagaina mention the eggs are soon to hatch; Nagaina snuck up behind Rikki.*

After Twenty Years

p. 190 Reading Strategy: Students should circle *the man* and *spoke*. Students should then use lines to separate the beginning and end of the sentence.

p. 190 Stop to Reflect: The man wants to ease the concern of the police officer that he might be there for criminal reasons.

p. 190 Read Fluently: Students should circle *Jimmy Wells, my best chum, and the finest chap in the world.*

p. 191 Reading Check: Students should circle *to make my fortune.*

p. 191 Literary Analysis: The police officer may be Jimmy Wells.

p. 191 Reading Check: Students should circle *I've had to compete with some of the sharpest wits going to get my pile . . .*

p. 192 Literary Analysis: Students should circle *with collar turned up to his ears.* This may mean the man is not Jimmy Wells.

p. 192 Stop to Reflect: (c) Both a and b seem likely.

p. 193 Literary Analysis: Most students will be surprised by this ending. The ending makes sense because it allows Jimmy to do his duty by having Bob arrested, while not making himself arrest his old friend.

Review and Assess

1. Bob and Jimmy agreed to meet at a specific time and place.

2. (b) They were close in childhood but have taken different paths in life.

3. Students should check *He wants to keep a promise . . . , He wants to show off . . . , He is curious . . .*

4. Jimmy is unable to arrest Bob himself because of the friendship and bond they once had.

5. Jimmy recognizes Bob as a criminal, the reader learns that Jimmy is the police officer, and Jimmy has another officer pose as himself to arrest Bob.

6. The police officer knows about the restaurant and when it was torn down; The police officer is probing Bob for details of his success out west.

7. Students should circle *a man leaned.* Students should draw lines between *store* and *a*, and between *leaned* and *with*. The man leaned in the doorway of a darkened hardware store. An unlit cigar was in his mouth.

Papa's Parrot

p. 198 Stop to Reflect: Students should circle *Though* and *merely.* (b) Harry's

p. 198 Reading Strategy: Students should answer yes. Harry is making friends and becoming interested in things other than the candy store.

p. 199 Literary Analysis: Students should circle *embarrassed* and label it *D*. Students should circle *he keeps walking* and label it *I*.

p. 199 Reading Check: Students should circle all words in quotation marks. Students should label *H* any phrase followed by *Harry said* or *Harry mumbled.* Students should label the other circled words *R*.

p. 200 Reading Fluently: (a) annoyed

p. 200 Stop to Reflect: His father

Review and Assess

1. Students should check *He has outgrown the store . . . , He and his friends now . . . , He is embarrassed . . .*

2. (d)

3. Harry learns that his father is lonely and misses him.

4. Students should write *Harry Tillian liked his papa.* Students should write *Mr. Tillian looked forward to seeing his son.*

5. Students should write *he keeps walking.* Students should write *Harry had always stopped in to see his father at work.*

6. Students should write *yes* or *no* and explain their responses.

Ribbons

p. 205 Read Fluently: Students should circle *She's here! She's here!* and *"Paw-paw's here!"*

p. 205 Reading Check: Students should circle *Chinese for grandmother.* Students should write *mother*

p. 205 Reading Strategy: Students should circle *What's wrong with her feet?* Students might ask *Why is she sensitive?*

p. 206 Reading Check: Ballet Lessons; her room

p. 206 Stop to Reflect: Answers will vary.

p. 207 Literary Analysis: Students should circle *Grandmother is a hero.*

p. 207 Reading Strategy: Students might ask *Why didn't the mother explain the ribbons to the grandmother?*

p. 208 Think Ahead: That something is wrong with Grandmother's feet.

p. 208 Reading Strategy: Students should circle *What happened to your feet?* Students might ask *Was that very painful?*

p. 208 Literary Analysis: (a) People try to spare their loved ones from pain.

p. 209 Literary Analysis: Students should check *People will undergo . . . , People will do painful things . . .*

p. 209 Stop to Reflect: The invisible ribbon is a bond between the women.

Review and Assess

1. Students should check *Grandmother is a brave woman . . . , Grandmother values freedom . . .*

2. (d) She can talk more with Ian, who has learned more Chinese.

3. Grandmother thinks the ribbons are for binding Stacy's feet.

4. (d) the loving family ties between Stacy, her mother, and Grandmother.

5. Students should check *Love and understanding . . . , We don't want those we love . . . , The best way to know a person . . .*

6. Students may ask questions such as *Why is grandmother so secretive? Because she is trying to shield her granddaughter. Why does grandmother treat Stacy differently than Ian? Because that is Chinese culture. What did grandmother's feet look like? Deformed.*

The Treasure of Lemon Brown

p. 214 Reading Check: Students should circle *dark* or *angry.* Students should circle (b) His father won't let him join the Scorpions.

p. 214 Reading Strategy: Answers will vary. *Is Greg afraid to be in the building?*

p. 215 Stop to Reflect: Students may say that Greg's father was trying to encourage Greg to work hard.

p. 215 Read Fluently: Students should circle (a) He fears being attacked.

p. 215 Reading Strategy: Students will have varying questions.

p. 216 Reading Strategy: Students will have varying questions. *How old is he?*

p. 216 Literary Analysis: Students should circle *Every man got a treasure. You don't know that, you must be a fool!*

p. 216 Stop to Reflect: Students should circle *No.* Students should circle *You got any money?*

p. 217 Think Ahead: Answers will vary. *Greg will make scary sounds.*

p. 217 Read Fluently: (c) proud

p. 217 Literary Analysis: Students should circle *Brown felt like his son would be able to do something since he knew his father had.* (c) Greg's father telling how he studied hard to pass the postal test.

p. 218 Literary Analysis: Students should circle (b) We often work harder for those we love.

p. 218 Stop to Reflect: Lemon's experiences may allow Greg to realize the accomplishments of his father and will bring Greg and his dad closer together.

p. 219 Stop to Reflect: Possible response: Greg smiles because he can now appreciate his father's lecture. He is looking forward to listening to his father.

Review and Assess

1. (d) He is blocks from home, and the rain is very heavy.

2. (c) They have heard that Brown has a treasure and want to steal it.

3. poor: homeless/lives in empty old building; dresses in rags

talented: got good reviews for playing harmonica and singing blues

loved family: traveled all over, working hard, to support his wife and son

proud: gave clippings of reviews of his performances to his son

sad: grieves for loss of wife and son

4. his old harmonica and clippings of old reviews of his performances

5. Students should put a check in front of *A person's achievements are a treasure that can be passed down* and *Just about everyone has a treasure of some kind.*

6. Possible question: What is Lemon Brown's treasure? Answer: an old harmonica he used to play when he performed, and clippings of old reviews of his performances

Possible question: Why does the treasure have special meaning to him? Answer: He gave it to his son, who treasured it and had it with him when he was killed in the war.

Possible question: What does Greg learn from Lemon Brown? Answer: to value his father's proud achievements and concern for Greg

Unit 7

I Am a Native of North America

p. 224 Reading Check: The entire family lived in grandfather's house.

p. 224 Reading Check: People learned to live with one another; learned to help one another; learned to respect the rights of one another.

p. 225 Reading Strategy: Students should circle *They stripped the land and poisoned the water and air.*

p. 225 Stop to Reflect: If we do not show love completely we are no better than the lowest of all animals. Answers will vary. Possible response: The ability to love is a special gift and if we choose not to use it we have refused the greatest gift of being human.

p. 225 Literary Analysis: Without love we become weak.

p. 226 Stop to Reflect: Answers will vary. In a perfect world this would make sense but it does not seem possible in the real modern day environment.

p. 226 Reading Strategy: Students should write *Many young people have forgotten the old ways. They have been made to feel ashamed of their Indian ways.*

p. 226 Reading Check: Native Americans must forgive the terrible sufferings the white society brought.

Review and Assess

1. Native American and White Society

2. Native Americans view nature as a gift that should be respected.

3. The author's idea of brotherhood is love and forgiveness.

4. Under *Native American Culture* students should write *People learn to respect the rights of their neighbors through communal living; People love and respect nature.* Under *White Society* students should write *People live near one another but do not know or care about their neighbors; People abuse nature.*

5. The author provided support for his main idea by explaining how well the Native American culture lived. He compares how the Native Americans used their natural resources to how the white society abused them.

All Together Now

p. 231 Reading Check: Individuals can solve the race problem in America by being more tolerant.

p. 231 Reading Check: No. People bring peace between races, not laws.

p. 231 Literary Analysis: Students should underline *Each of us can decide to have one friend of a different race or background.*

p. 232 Reading Strategy: Students should underline *Babies come into the world as blank as slates* and *Children learn ideas and attitudes from the adults*

p. 232 Literary Analysis: Students should circle *Parents can actively encourage their children to be in the company of people* *who are of other racial and ethnic backgrounds.*

p. 232 Stop to Reflect: It is easier to make small changes than it is to try to solve the whole problem.

Review and Assess

1. people
2. Civil Rights Act of 1964; Voting Rights Act of 1965. Laws cannot create tolerance; people's attitudes have to change.
3. The author means babies are innocent and can be taught anything by their parents and teachers.
4. The author is dedicated to bringing people together. She wants people to work towards racial peace.
5. Possible response: Do the supporting details make sense? Do they persuade me to accept the author's point of view? Students' responses to the second question may vary, but they should explain their answers.

How to Enjoy Poetry

p. 237 Literary Analysis: Students should underline *When you really feel it, a new part of you happens, or an old part is renewed, with surprise and delight at being what it is.*

p. 237 Reading Check: Things; actions; feelings

p. 237 Reading Check: Poetry comes to you from outside you.

p. 238 Reading Strategy: Students should underline *Poetry can describe the sun and stars in different ways and from different perspectives.*

p. 238 Literary Analysis: Dickey explains how to begin writing poetry.

p. 238 Reading Strategy: (b) It hints at the way a poem flows, or sounds, when you read it. Students should explain their responses.

p. 239 Literary Analysis: Students should underline *Almost anything put into rhythm and rhyme is more memorable than the same thing said in prose.*

p. 239 Stop to Reflect: Yes. Both reading and writing poetry help you to look at your own life differently. Reading and writing poetry help you make connections between things that you have never connected before.

Review and Assess

1. (c) poetry comes to you from outside you and something from within you must meet it
2. Giving to poetry means allowing yourself to get into the words and feel their meanings.
3. Rhythm and rhyme are important to poetry because they make the words more memorable and more pleasant to read.
4. Dickey explains that poetry can uncover a new part of you, and he explains how poetry comes to you from the outside.
5. 1. When you really feel poetry, a new part of you happens. 2. To understand poetry is to know it comes to you from outside. 3. You must make a gut connection with the poetry.

"The Chase" *from* An American Childhood

p. 244 Literary Analysis: Students should circle *all out* and *Your fate . . . depended on your concentration and courage.*

p. 244 Reading Strategy: The author wants the reader to know she enjoys competition and sports.

p. 244 Reading Check: The black car stops because it was hit with snowballs.

p. 245 Reading Strategy: Students should circle *He was in city clothes: a suit and tie, street shoes.* The purpose for including this information is to describe the challenge this driver took on when he decided to chase the kids in the snow.

p. 245 Literary Analysis: Students should underline *You have to throw yourself into an activity with all of your energy if you want to win.*

p. 245 Stop to Reflect: Students answers will vary.

p. 246 Literary Analysis: Dillard's description of the events tells us she enjoys challenges and seeks excitement.

p. 246 Reading Strategy: Dillard wants to show the level of difficulty and the toll the chase has taken on the pursuer.

p. 246 Literary Analysis: Students should underline *The point was that he chased us passionately without giving up, and so he had caught us.*

p. 247 Reading Check: Dillard feels the most satisfying thing about her experience is that she went all out and did her very best in a challenging situation.

Review and Assess

1. Dillard enjoys the competition and mental and physical aspects of football.
2. Dillard is outgoing. Dillard is competitive.

3. Dillard feels the man was a worthy opponent. She tells us this by describing how difficult the chase was for everyone involved.
4. A passage that entertains: *He ran after us, and we ran away . . . we were running for our lives.* A passage that teaches a lesson: *Then she realized that the man knew the same thing she did: You have to throw yourself into an activity with all your energy if you want to win.* A passage that explains something about the author: *Your fate . . . Nothing girls did could compare to it.*

Unit 8

A Christmas Carol: Scrooge and Marley, Act 1, Scenes 1 & 2

p. 252 Reading Strategy: Students should respond with their own ideas of what a ghost looks like.

p. 252 Vocabulary: (b) joke

p. 253 Vocabulary: A poulterer sells poultry.

p. 253 Reading Check: The story takes place on Christmas Eve, 1843.

p. 253 Read Fluently: Make sure that students can pronounce all the words in the speech. Explain any words they don't understand.

p. 254 Reading Strategy: Students should circle *ancient, awful, dead-eyed*

p. 254 Reading Strategy: Students may say that Scrooge might jump or open his eyes and mouth wide.

p. 254 Reading Check: He doesn't think his nephew should be merry because he is poor.

p. 254 Literary Analysis: Bah! Humbug!

p. 255 Stop to Reflect: (c) making money

p. 255 Reading Check: Students should underline *But Scrooge rudely refuses.*

p. 255 Reading Strategy: Students should draw a diagram that reflects the scene.

p. 256 Literary Analysis: Students should circle *Cratchit smiles faintly.*

p. 256 Reading Check: Cratchit gets one day off a year.

p. 256 Reading Check: Cratchit wants to say Merry Christmas. Scrooge hates Christmas.

p. 256 Reading Strategy: The scenery changes from an office to a street scene. Music is heard. People walk by.

p. 257 Literary Analysis: Possible response: Scrooge is grumpy and snaps at passing boys. The other characters are happy and cheerful.

Review and Assess

1. Jacob Marley is Scrooge's former business partner. He is a ghost in this play.
2. Scenes 1 and 2 take place in Scrooge's place of business, a countinghouse.
3. Scrooge is stingy and he doesn't want to pay Cratchit for a day when he doesn't work.
4. *Things Scrooge Says:*

   Bah! Humbug!

   Every idiot who goes about with "Merry Christmas" on his lips, should be boiled with his own pudding, and buried with a stake of holly through his heart.

   Things Scrooge Does:

   He refuses to go to his nephew's for Christmas dinner.

   He refuses to give the kind men a donation for the poor.
5. *How he moves:* Possible response: He walks slowly, with a cane. He is bent over.

   His facial expressions: Possible response: He frowns. He says mean things under his breath. He tries to hit people with his cane.

A Christmas Carol: Scrooge and Marley, Act 1, Scenes 3–5

p. 262 Reading Check: He sees Jacob Marley's face on the door knocker.

p. 262 Reading Strategy: Students should circle *horrible to look at, pigtail, vest, suit as usual, drags an enormous chain, is transparent*

p. 262 Reading Check: cash-boxes, keys, padlocks, ledgers, deeds, heavy purses of steel. Possible response: All Marley cared about in life was money, so he has to drag these things around as a punishment.

p. 263 Literary Analysis: Students should draw a sketch of the scene as it is described.

p. 263 Reading Check: He screams a ghostly scream and takes off his head.

p. 263 Stop to Reflect: He did not care for other people during his life. All he cared about was money.

p. 263 Reading Strategy: Students should use their imaginations to picture this figure. Possible response: A child with the head of an old man.

p. 264 Literary Analysis: Students should circle the words *sir, really, please do understand*

p. 264 Literary Analysis: Students should circle *panicked*

p. 264 Reading Strategy: It is a snowy day in the country.

p. 265 Reading Check: Students should underline *he thinks of the young caroler whom he shooed away from his office earlier that night. He says he wishes he had given him something.*

p. 265 Reading Check: He thinks about Cratchit. He wishes that he had been kinder to him.

p. 265 Reading Strategy: They describe how the boy Ebenezer is replaced by a man Ebenezer. The co-workers disappear and a young woman in mourning clothes appears.

p. 266 Reading Check: money

p. 266 Reading Check: The world is hard on people who are poor and it punishes people who try to be rich.

p. 266 Stop to Reflect: He wishes that he had done things differently.

p. 267 Reading Check: She is releasing him from marrying her.

p. 267 Stop to Reflect: Answers will vary. Students should describe something happy that they want to see again.

p. 267 Reading Check: The ghost of Christmas Past appears, Scrooge sees himself as a lonely boy in the schoolhouse. Scrooge sees his former boss and coworkers. Scrooge sees himself and a woman.

Review and Assess

1. Marley's ghost has to carry the chain because he didn't care for other people in life.

2. The Ghost of Christmas Past visits Scrooge after Marley leaves.

3. Scrooge as a young boy: Scrooge cries.
   Scrooge as a twelve-year-old boy: He says he loved his sister.
   Scrooge with his coworkers: He wishes he had been kinder to Cratchit.
   Scrooge with his fiancée: He yells "No!"

4. Scrooge was a lonely boy. Scrooge had a sister whom he loved. Scrooge was engaged at one time.

5. He panics.

Unit 9

The Cremation of Sam McGee

p. 272 Reading Strategy: Students should underline *it stabbed like a driven nail.* The cold air is being compared to a driven nail as it stabs through the parka into the body.

p. 272 Reading Check: Sam McGee was miserable because he was from the south and wasn't used to cold weather.

p. 272 Reading Strategy: Students should circle *chilled clean through to the bone.*

p. 272 Reading Check: Last remains refers to a dead body.

p. 273 Literary Analysis: Sam dies from the cold.

p. 273 Stop to Reflect: Possible response: The fire may warm Sam back to life.

p. 273 Literary Analysis: Students should circle *snow* and *know*. Students should draw a box around *fear* and *near*. Student should draw arrows from *out* to *about*; from *dread* to *said*; from *cooked* to *looked*; and from *wide* to *inside*.

p. 274 Literary Analysis: Students should check *Character*, *Setting*, and *Plot*. Sam the *character* is speaking, the cold *setting* is described, and the *plot* is covered by Sam speaking and the narration.

Review and Assess

1. unbearably cold
2. He is trying to earn money.
3. He promises to cremate Sam's body.
4. Sam felt so bad, the narrator felt obligated to keep his promise.
5. Sam McGee sitting up getting warm.
6. 1. setting: The cold Arctic. 2. characters: Sam McGee. 3. rhythm: Well he seemed so low that I couldn't say no.
7. Students should complete the *What it means* part with *it was unbearably cold; a very bright smile;* and *I tried not to be afraid.*

Annabel Lee

p. 279 Reading Check: She died from the cold.

p. 279 Literary Analysis: Students should circle *me*, *sea*, *chilling*, *killing*, and *Lee*.

p. 279 Reading Strategy: The moon and stars remind me of Annabel Lee.

p, 279 Literary Analysis: Students should read the bracketed lines aloud putting emphasis on the underlined words.

p. 280 Stop to Reflect: 1. Lonely. 2. Angry. 3. Bitter

Review and Assess

1. The narrator blames the angels and the cold for Annabel Lee's death. The narrator believes the angels were jealous of the love between him and Annabel.
2. The narrator talks about the sea because the young lovers lived near the sea.
3. Students should underline *love*, *stronger far*, *love those*, *older*, *we*, *many*, *wiser*, and *we*
4. Students should list *beams/dreams*,

rise/eyes, sea/Lee, and *nighttide/bride/side* as the sets of rhyming words in the final stanza.

5. The moon and stars remind me of Annabel Lee.

Maestro

p. 285 Reading Strategy: *Upturned* means to be facing upwards. Students should write the words *turned up*.

p. 285 Reading Check: He hears his mother's voice.

p. 285 Stop to Reflect: A song can be sung so beautifully that one might describe it as tasting great rather than sounding great. *Sweet on the tongue* is an example of this.

Review and Assess

1. The voice, the guitar, and the violin.
2. Sentimental, happy, proud.
3. Students should circle the word *strummed*.
4. Under *Clues that help Clarify*, students should write *in the air; to snare*. Beneath *Clarified Meaning*, students should write *to be tossed up in the air.*

The Village Blacksmith

p. 290 Literary Analysis: Students should circle *his brawny arms are strong as iron bands.* This comparison tells us that the blacksmith has great strength.

p. 290 Reading Strategy: Students should circle the words *he hears the parson pray and preach, he hears his daughter's voice.*

p. 290 Reading Check: The blacksmith cries because he is remembering his wife who has passed away.

p. 291 Stop to Reflect: Human lives often involve hard work under difficult circumstances and conditions. A hard fought life can be rewarding also like the work of the blacksmith.

Review and Assess

1. The blacksmith's life is difficult. His daily work involves dealing with extreme heat and lifting heavy materials.
2. Rough; large; strong.
3. His daughter singing reminds the blacksmith of his dead wife.

4. The correct answer is a furnace.
5. In the spaces under *Sense*, students should write *Sight; Touch; Sound*. In the spaces under *Sensory Language*, students should write *Spreading chestnut tree; Strong as iron hands; He hears the parson pray and preach.*

Unit 10

Popocatepetl and Ixtlaccihuatl

p. 296 Reading Check: Tenochtitlan

p. 297 Reading Strategy: Students should read ahead to see if the Emperor makes wise decisions.

p. 297 Reading Check: Students should underline *forbade her to marry.*

p. 297 Reading Check: The Emperor trusted no one.

p. 298 Reading Strategy: Answers will vary. The Emperor must have had wisdom to rule for so long. The Emperor never had wisdom if he forbade his daughter to marry.

p. 298 Reading Check: As a reward, the emperor offers the hand of his daughter and the equal right to reign and rule Tenochtitlan.

p. 298 Literary Analysis: Aztecs regarded warriors as heroes and war as a battle for honor.

p. 298 Reading Check: The warriors report false news because they were jealous of Popo's success.

p. 299 Reading Check: Ixtla dies because she believes her love has been killed in battle.

p. 299 Reading Strategy: Student should read ahead to find details about Popo that make him more than an ordinary man.

p. 299 Literary Analysis: The warriors could not have built the pyramid in one day. This is part of the folk tale that makes it sound miraculous.

p. 299 Reading Check: He carried her body to the top of the pyramid and buried it under a heap of stones.

p. 300 Literary Analysis: Students should check *Popo had two pyramids . . .* , *Popo stood next to Ixtla's . . .*

p. 300 Stop to Reflect: No. This is an Aztec folk tale that was written as a fictional account of the mountains' origins.

Review and Assess

1. The emperor forbids them to marry.
2. By offering his daughter as a reward, he does not recognize her wishes.
3. Students should circle (a) The kingdom ends up with no ruler.
4. Ixtla dies because she believes the man she loves has been killed in battle.
5. Reading ahead sometimes helps you better understand what is happening earlier.
6. Possible responses: smoke in the memory of the princess; pyramids that change to volcanoes; Popo's decision to stand on top of the pyramid forever.

The People Could Fly

p. 305 Reading Strategy: Students should underline *people who could fly; magic of flying; slavery; slave ships*, and *dark-skinned.*

p. 305 Reading Check: The people are full of misery because they can't fly any more. They are miserable because they have been enslaved.

p. 305 Reading Check: Some people have the special gift of being able to fly.

p. 306 Literary Analysis: Students should circle the words *call him Toby; standin'*, and *Now.*

p. 306 Reading Check: Sarah can't feed her baby because the overseer is watching.

p. 306 Reading Strategy: Possible responses: violence; abuse; treating people and babies badly.

p. 307 Literary Analysis: Students should underline *said so quickly* and *sounded like whispers and sighs.*

p. 307 Reading Check: Possible response: The master wants to kill Toby because Toby is helping slaves escape.

p. 307 Reading Check: The magic words are *buba yali* and *buba tambe.*

p. 308 Literary Analysis: The correct answer is *B*.

p. 308 Stop to Reflect: Most students will say it inspires hope because people find a way to save themselves from violence and pain.

Review and Assess

1. The people lose their wings when they become slaves.
2. Sarah tells Toby she must leave soon because she thought she would die.
3. Toby helps Sarah by chanting a spell and helping her fly.
4. Possible responses include: *say; hollerin',* and *Couldn't believe it, call him Toby; standin', Call her Sarah,* and *Now.*
5. *Life was painful and hard. They wanted to be free and they wanted to be safe.*

Demeter and Persephone

p. 313 Literary Analysis: The events might describe volcanic eruptions.

p. 313 Reading Strategy: Eros will shoot an arrow and someone will fall in love. Some students may predict that this love will stop the monsters from shaking the earth.

p. 314 Literary Analysis: The Greeks say that people are hit by Eros' arrow and fall in love.

p. 314 Reading Check: Students should underline *Eros shoots an arrow straight into Pluto's heart* and *a young woman gathering flowers.*

p. 314 Reading Check: Persephone is the daughter of Demeter, the goddess of the harvest. Pluto kidnaps Persephone.

p. 315 Reading Strategy: Possible response: Demeter might set the world on fire or destroy it.

p. 315 Literary Analysis: The ancient Greeks believed that natural disasters were caused by the gods.

p. 315 Reading Strategy: Students may predict that Zeus will save Persephone.

p. 315 Reading Check: tasted food in the realm of the dead.

p. 316 Reading Check: She likes things with fragrance. Jewels have no fragrance.

p. 316 Reading Strategy: Students may predict that Persephone will be very unhappy or that she will die.

p. 316 Literary Analysis: We have winter because Demeter doesn't allow things to grow while her daughter, Persephone, is with Pluto.

Review and Assess

1. Pluto takes Persephone to his kingdom because he is in love with her.
2. The correct answer is *C*.
3. Zeus solves the problem by asking Hermes to bring Persephone back.
4. When Persephone is on earth, there is spring and summer. When she is in the underworld the earth has fall and winter.
5. The myth of Demeter and Persephone explains the cycle of the seasons.
6. Possible responses: **Persephone:** *Prediction:* Students may have predicted she would die. *Outcome:* She did not die; but she was not completely happy either. **Demeter:** *Prediction:* Students may have predicted that Demeter would get Persephone back. *Outcome:* Demeter was able to get Persephone back for part of the year.

Icarus and Daedalus

p. 321 Reading Check: Students should circle *a wonderful Labyrinth.*

p. 321 Reading Check: It seemed impossible to leave because every ship was guarded.

p. 321 Reading Strategy: Students should say what they think Daedalus will do.

p. 322 Literary Analysis: He tries to teach Icarus how to use the wings safely.

p. 322 Reading Strategy: If he doesn't remember his father's instructions he might be badly hurt or even die.

p. 322 Reading Strategy: The heat of the sun could melt his feathers apart.

p. 323 Reading Check: Students should underline the following: *The heat of the sun had melted the wax from his wings; the feathers were falling.*

p. 323 Stop to Reflect: Students should say what they would do in the same situation.

Review and Assess

1. He is in Crete.

2. He plans to create wings so he can fly away.

3. He warns him not to fly too low or too high.

4. Icarus drowns at the end of the myth.

5. The myth teaches us the importance of being careful and cautious, and it teaches us to pay attention to others when they are teaching us how to do something that can be dangerous.

The following are some clues from the story: "For Icarus, these cautions went in at one ear and out by the other." / Icarus forgets all the instructions and soars as high as he can. / His father is way below him.

Answers to Part 2

Burning Out at Nine?

p. 329 Read Fluently: Students should underline three of the following "He wakes up at 6 every weekday morning," "downs a five minute breakfast," "reports to school at 7:50," "returns home at 3:15," "hits the books from 5 to 9," and "goes to sleep at 10:30."

p. 329 Reading Strategy: The author thinks that children's schedules are too busy. Students should circle "Remember when enjoying life seemed like the point of childhood? Huh!"

p. 330 Reading Magazine Articles: Most students will agree that the information is not up-to-date because it was written in 1998.

p. 330 Reading Strategy: The use of experts' opinions strengthens the author's argument by giving the impression that what the author says is true.

p. 330 Reading Check: The average child spends 12 hours a week in unstructured play.

p. 331 Reading Informational Materials: The story does not mention the opinions of experts or parents who think that children today have enough leisure time. It also doesn't mention the opinions of those who think that children have too much leisure time.

p. 332 Review and Assess

Check Your Comprehension

1. Children's leisure time is defined as time left over after sleeping, eating, personal hygiene, and attending school or day care.

2. Unstructured play encourages independent thinking and allows children to negotiate relationships with their peers.

3. (a) The amount of time children spend watching television has dropped by 25 percent. (b) The amount of time children spend reading has changed very little.

Applying the Reading Strategy

4. They show mostly negative effects of busy schedules for children.

5. Possible response: Children's busy schedules are having a negative effect on their health and happiness.

Writing Informational Materials

Possible sources of information include the Internet, magazines, newspapers, and interviews.

Golden Girls

p. 334 Reading Strategy: Students may underline any of the following: "the lumps in their throats," "the chills that ran down their spines," "the eye-dampening sight," "high-stepping," "a steadily building roar of oh-oh-ooOOHH!" and the quote by A. J. Mleczko. These words suggest that the author is happy about the victory and can relate to the team's feelings of excitement and emotion.

p. 334 Reading Check: Sandra Whyte scored the last goal.

p. 335 Reading Strategy: Students should circle "(b) admiring." An example that supports the attitude might be the author's description of the "saves, many of them spectacular."

p. 335 Read Fluently: Students should circle the word "grousing"; students should underline the word "gushing."

p. 335 Reading Informational Materials:
The quotations support the author's attitude and also add interest because they contain the exact words of real people.

p. 336 Review and Assess
Comprehension Check

1. (a) Her dream was to play on the U.S. national soccer team. (b) She had not received an invitation to try out for the team.

2. This victory could give other female athletes hope for future performances and victories.

Applying the Reading Strategy

3. It suggests that she admires the team members and respects their talent.

4. She thinks that women are up to the challenge of playing "grittier" sports if given the opportunity. She says this in the concluding paragraph of the article.

Writing Informational Materials
Possible response:

1. How did it feel to win the gold medal?

2. What other teams did you have to beat to get to the finals?

3. Do you plan to keep playing hockey?

Memos

p. 338 Reading Strategy: You can locate the subject under "RE:" The subject is photo identification cards.

p. 338 Reading Check: Students should underline "All the new employees, anyone who is missing their picture on their employee identification badge."

p. 338 Read Fluently: The deadline is 12/15/00.

p. 338 Reading Informational Materials:
The headings come first. The first paragraph contains the most important information. Other details follow. The paragraphs are set up in block style. Each paragraph discusses one thing in direct language. The format works well because the information can be read quickly by employees, and they will know exactly what to do.

p. 339 Review and Assess
Check Your Comprehension

1. They can continue to use their badges for two weeks.

2. They need the badges to enter the building.

Applying the Reading Strategy

3. Answer: John Charles, Facilities Manager
Abbreviation or heading: FR
Answer: 12/1/00
Abbreviation or heading: DATE
Answer: Photo Ids
Abbreviation or heading: RE
Answer: All Employees at Needham Facility
Abbreviation or heading: TO
Answer: Captain Schaeffer, Security Chief; Don Rolds, USR Facilities Manager; Linda O'Connell, director of Human Resources
Abbreviation or heading: cc

4. a map to the security office

Writing Informational Materials
Possible response:
TO: All students in Mrs. Johnson's 4th period English class
FR: John Doe
DATE: 01/31/04
RE: Car Wash
CC: Mrs. Johnson, Principal Greenstone
Encl: Advertising Flier
On March 3 from 1pm to 5pm our class will hold a car wash at the gas station on the corner of Elm and Locust. Please bring a rag and a bucket with you.
Post the enclosed flier in your neighborhood.

A Colony in the Sky

p. 341 Reading Magazine Articles: The topic is the colonization of Mars.

p. 341 Read Fluently:

1. The more we know about the solar system's other planets, the better we will understand Earth.

2. This will make us safer.

p. 342 Reading Check:
Students may choose three of the following: general size, presence of water, length of days, or range of temperatures.

p. 342 Reading Strategy: Students should circle the word "recipe."

p. 343 Reading Strategy: Students may name two of the following: growing a garden, creating a wilderness, building a cathedral, or flying seeds over an ocean to drop them on a new island.

p. 343 Stop to Reflect: Students may say that terraforming Mars is a good idea because it will help us learn more about Earth. Others may say it is not a good idea because it is not possible. Answers will vary, but they should include valid reasons.

p. 343 Reading Informational Materials: Possible responses:
1. *Discover*
2. *National Geographic*
3. a science magazine
4. a magazine for school children

p. 344 Review and Assess

Check Your Comprehension

1. Mars resembles Earth in its size, presence of water, length of day, and range of temperatures.
2. "To terraform" means to alter Mars's surface to make it able to sustain Earth's plants and animals. It would require adding nitrogen, oxygen, and water as well as importing Earth's life forms. In addition, it would take centuries to form.

Applying the Reading Strategy

3. The analogy presents a difficult concept—terraforming—by comparing it to a familiar concept—cooking. Relating it to a simple concept helps readers understand the thinking behind the unfamiliar process and helps relieve fears of the process.
4. (a) The writer compares the colonization of Mars to a giant laboratory or university. (b) The items being compared are the colonization of Mars and a laboratory/university. Both are sites of experiments and places of learning.

Writing Informational Materials

Possible responses:

Planting a seed is like burying treasure. Cutting the grass is like giving the Earth a haircut. Healthy eating is like putting the proper kind of gasoline in your car.

Algal Blooms

p. 346 Reading Textbooks: Possible response: It is helpful to include a picture because readers may not know what an algal bloom is or what it looks like.

p. 346 Reading Check: They found toxins.

p. 347 Reading Textbooks: Students should underline "the algae that grow rapidly . . . turn the color of the water red."

p. 347 Read Fluently: Possible response: When there is an increase in the amount of nutrients in the water, red tides will occur more frequently.

p. 347 Reading Strategy: People may become seriously ill.

p. 348 Reading Textbooks: Possible response: If you didn't know the answer to the Check Point question, you could go back and reread the selection in order to find the answer.

p. 348 Reading Informational Materials: The feature is the heading "Integrating Technology." This heading helps readers locate specific information quickly.

p. 349 Review and Assess

Check Your Comprehension

1. Some whales died because they consumed toxic algae and fish.
2. An algal bloom is the rapid growth of a population of algae.

Applying the Reading Strategy

3. An increase in nutrients in the water, an increase in water temperature, and seasonal changes can cause red tides.
4. Technology enables scientists to track how red tides move and to detect increases in ocean temperature.

Using Informational Material

Possible response:

1. This literature textbook is organized into units.
2. The images visually show the subject matter of the selections. They also make the textbook more interesting.
3. This textbook uses headings, subheadings, and checkpoint questions to call out important information.

How Do Rainmakers Make It Rain ?

p. 351 Reading Essays: Possible response: A question can indicate a cause-and-effect relationship. The question in the title of this essay shows that the essay will explore the causes of rain.

p. 351 Read Fluently: Some clouds do not produce rain because the particles of water never grow large enough to fall to the ground as rain.

p. 352 Reading Check: The effect is that pure water in supercooled clouds does not freeze even when its temperature is below the freezing point. Students should circle the phrase "But the water can be 10 or 20 degrees below freezing (supercooled) without actually freezing."

p. 352 Reading Strategy:

1. 70 mm guns fire silver iodide particles at supercooled clouds.

2. Explosions spread the silver iodide particles at the right height.

3. Silver iodide helps water particles freeze and grow large.

4. When the particles become heavy enough, they fall to the ground as rain.

p. 352 Reading Informational Materials: The clouds must be supercooled in order to produce increased rainfall.

p. 353 Review and Assess

Check Your Comprehension

1. Clouds are made of tiny particles of water.

2. Small droplets of rain evaporate before they reach the ground.

3. Silver iodide particles have been dropped from aircraft, carried by rockets, fired by guns, or released at ground level so air currents could carry them into the atmosphere.

Applying the Reading Strategy

4. Most students will choose the cause-and-effect relationship in which a single cause triggers a series of events. For instance, firing silver iodide particles at clouds triggers a series of events that result in falling rain.

5. It is important for a writer to choose a cause-and-effect relationship before writing in order to reach a complete understanding of how events are connected. This knowledge allows the writer to explain these relationships more clearly to an audience.

Writing Informational Materials

Students should choose a historical topic and a type of cause-and-effect organization before writing their essays. A variety of cause-and-effect organizations are valid for historical topics. For example, the suggested topic, the American Revolution, could be represented chronologically as a chain of events. Or it could be seen as a multitude of causes (the Stamp Act, the lack of representation in English Parliament, etc.) producing a single effect. Students should consistently apply their chosen organization to their essays.

Signs

p. 355 Reading Signs: The most important information is the name of The National Oregon Trail Center. It is in the biggest and boldest type.

p. 355 Read Fluently: Students should circle "5:00 PM."

p. 355 Reading Strategy: Your purpose might be to find out about special group times and rates. The sign tells you whom to call to get the information you need.

p. 356 Reading Strategy: A hiker might want to know what happened at the site.

p. 356 Stop to Reflect: Possible answer: You might find a historical sign at a museum or a historic landmark.

p. 356 Reading Informational Materials:
First sign
1. hours of operation
2. cost to visit
3. who to contact to set up school trips
Second sign
1. what happened at the site
2. who is buried there

p. 357 Review and Assess

Check Your Comprehension

1. The Trail Center opens at 10:00 A.M.

2. Ormond Alford, his sons William M. Alford and Lorenzo D. Alford, and John W. Cameron, a friend, are buried there.

Applying the Reading Strategy

3. Possible response: When is it open? Are tours available? How much does it cost to visit?

4. The physical arrangement of information about times, the word *tours*, and a list of admission prices would help a visitor find that information.

Writing Informational Materials

Students will probably put the name of the museum in the largest type. Other information should include the hours of operation, the cost of visiting, special arrangements, and special exhibits.

The Eternal Frontier

p. 359 Reading Essays: The author asks, "Where is the frontier now?" The author will support his position that the frontier lies in outer space.

p. 359 Read Fluently: Possible response: By citing statistics and numerical facts, L'Amour supports his position that the new frontier is outer space. He cites statistics to show that the earth is overpopulated and overdeveloped, supporting his position that space exploration is a good idea.

p. 360 Reading Strategy: Possible response: The author's main purpose is to convince readers of the need to explore outer space. Students may underline any of the following: "Mankind is not bound by its atmospheric envelope . . . by any limits at all," "It is our destiny to move out . . . to dare the unknown," "It is our destiny to achieve," "Yet we must not forget . . . did not exist before," or "The computer age has arisen . . . of computing devices."

p. 360 Reading Informational Materials: Possible response: This statement helps readers see L'Amour's point of view: If we do not explore new technologies and advances, we will never move forward or realize our full potential as a society.

p. 361 Review and Assess

Check Your Comprehension

1. L'Amour refers to outer space as the "eternal frontier."

2. He says we need leaders with perspective, "men and women who can take the long view and help to shape the outlines of our future."

Applying the Reading Strategy

3. Students should identify any of the facts and statistics L'Amour uses about past inventions, such as radio, automobiles, television, airplanes, electricity, and paving of roads, to show that humankind has been inventive on Earth and should pursue space exploration.

4. Some students may say that L'Amour achieves his purpose because he uses solid facts to support his point and is convincing. Other students may say he fails to achieve his purpose because he does not refute opposing arguments.

Writing Informational Materials

Tell students to use persuasive techniques such as emotional appeal, facts, and statistics to support their positions. Remind students that their arguments should be convincing and sound.

Walking for Exercise and Pleasure

p. 363 Reading Government Publications: Headings break up the text into more manageable sections; they give clues to the information in each section so that people can quickly find what they are looking for.

p. 363 Read Fluently: Students should circle "39.5%." This number represents the group of people that had the highest percentage of regular walkers: men 65 years of age or older.

p. 363 Stop to Reflect: Possible responses: People walk for pleasure, to relieve tension, for exercise, to get somewhere, or to be alone. Students may say that their parents or grandparents walk. They should give reasons.

p. 364 Reading Strategy: Students should choose four of the following:

1. Walking can improve the body's ability to consume oxygen.

2. It lowers a person's resting heart rate.

3. It reduces blood pressure.

4. It increases the efficiency of the heart and lungs.

5. It burns calories.

p. 364 Reading Check: Walking and running burn approximately the same amount of calories per mile. Running burns calories faster. Students should circle "Briskly walking one mile in 15 minutes burns just about the same number of calories as jogging an equal distance in 8 1/2 minutes."

p. 365 Reading Check:

1. It doesn't cost anything.
2. You can do it almost anytime and anywhere.
3. Almost anyone can do it.

p. 365 Reading Strategy: They are causes because they explain *why* walking is so popular.

p. 365 Reading Informational Materials: Students might point out the headings within the document, the bulleted list, the short paragraphs, or the clear, direct language.

p. 366 Review and Assess

Check Your Comprehension

1. Approximately one-half of Americans claim to exercise regularly.
2. Characteristics of an efficient walking style include holding the head erect, keeping the back straight and the abdomen flat, pointing the toes straight ahead, swinging the arms loosely at the sides, landing on the heel of the foot and rolling forward, taking long and easy strides, leaning forward when walking rapidly or walking up or down hills, and breathing deeply.

Applying the Reading Strategy

3. You should invest in a comfortable pair of shoes, walk with good posture and form, and walk regularly.
4. If you experience dizziness, nausea, or pain, you should slow down or stop walking.

Using Informational Materials

Students' paragraphs should reflect the information they learned in the publication. Remind students to describe several specific advantages of walking. Tell students that their persuasive arguments should be backed up with facts.

The Iceman

p. 368 Reading Primary Research: Lessem's main point is to describe Ötzi, the frozen man, and the objects found with him. Lessem explains that these objects show what Ötzi's life and times were like.

p. 368 Reading Check: Students should circle "Ötzi may have been a shepherd . . . in search of messages from gods."

p. 369 Reading Strategy: Possible response: The bow and arrow found with Ötzi indicate that he was an experienced hunter. Based on the fact that there was a forest on the other side of the mountain, it is possible that Ötzi had planned to go hunting.

p. 369 Read Fluently: Students should circle "hard flints" and "fine ax."

p. 369 Reading Primary Research: Students should note that the author bases his conclusion on the discovery of the flint and felt strips.

p. 370 Reading Strategy: Possible response: Ötzi died from the cold and snow. It took 5,000 years for his body to be discovered. Ötzi's belongings help people to better understand life during the Copper Age.

p. 370 Reading Informational Materials: Most students will probably agree that presenting evidence in the form of a story is very useful. It helps to put the evidence into context so that readers have a better understanding of the facts.

p. 371 Review and Assess

Check Your Comprehension

1. Ötzi's physical build indicates his strength, and his tattoos suggest that he may have been regarded as brave.
2. At such a high altitude, there were no twigs to burn.
3. If they searched, they would have found only a blanket of snow.

Applying the Reading Strategy

4. He had a finely crafted bow and arrows, as well as an ax.
5. Possible response: He froze to death because he could not build a fire. Because he was frozen, his body was preserved.

Using Informational Materials

Possible response: Primary research articles focus on information that has been acquired first-hand. Their purpose is to share new and unpublished information. The purpose of encyclopedias, however, is to categorize and relate all known information. Articles found in encyclopedias are based on information found in other articles and on primary research articles.

Let the Reader Beware

p. 378 Reading Guidelines: The title "Let the Reader Beware" refers to information on the Internet. The author is saying that information on the Internet frequently lacks credibility.

p. 378 Reading Strategy: The heading is a summary of the main idea of the paragraphs below it. Each heading is a tip for evaluating information on the Internet.

p. 379 Stop to Reflect: Students should indicate that the second meaning of *home page* is appropriate because the text refers to biographical information.

p. 379 Read Fluently: Possible response: The author warns readers about agendas because they can influence the quality of information presented on a site. A hidden agenda or bias could mean facts are omitted or an opposing side is not given its fair due.

p. 379 Reading Guidelines: Students should underline sentences that include the following phrases: "current information is usually more valid and useful than older material" and "check out some of its links."

p. 380 Reading Check: Students should circle the sentence "Ideally, you should confirm the information with at least two other sources." It is especially important to triangulate data if it runs counter to your understanding or if you are using the information for an important decision.

p. 380 Reading Informational Materials: It is useful to have boxes in guidelines in order to call readers' attention to information that is particularly useful.

p. 381 Review and Assess

Check Your Comprehension

1. Possible response: One danger is that the source of the information could be inaccurate or biased.

2. Information on the Internet can be verified by checking other reputable Web sites or by consulting print sources. The reader can also check the credentials of the author or organization who is posting the information on the Internet.

Applying the Reading Strategy

3. The introduction explains the purpose of the guidelines.

4. The numbered points summarize the main ideas and make the information easy to find.

5. The format of these guidelines does not follow a strict chronological order. Guidelines on how to access the Internet would have to follow a chronological, step-by-step order to be useful.

Using Informational Materials

Possible responses:

1. Guidelines for a research report assignment

2. Guidelines for how to handle an emergency situation

1. Guidelines for how to operate office equipment

2. Guidelines for taking sick days and vacation days

The Bill of Rights

p. 383 Reading Public Documents: Possible response: A document written today would be typed, not handwritten. It would be on regular white paper, not parchment paper.

p. 383 Reading Check: The Bill of Rights contains the first ten amendments to the Constitution.

p. 384 Reading Strategy: Check students' definitions of words.

p. 384 Read Fluently: Possible response: The accused has the right to a speedy trial with an impartial jury. The accused also has the right to be informed of his or her crime and to be represented by a lawyer.

p. 385 Reading Informational Materials: Direct wording leaves less room for misinterpretation or misunderstanding of the laws.

p. 386 Review and Assess

Check Your Comprehension

1. The First Amendment protects freedom of religion, speech, and the press.
2. The state or the people hold powers that the Constitution does not specifically give to the United States, according to the Tenth Amendment.

Applying the Reading Strategy

3. Students should summarize each amendment, as in the chart on p. 382.
4. Students should identify the unfamiliar words and look them up in a dictionary.

Writing Informational Materials

Students' revisions should indicate a clear understanding of the amendment and should be written in their own words.

Pandas

p. 388 Reading Research Reports: The main idea of this report is that the giant panda is a rare and special animal.

p. 388 Read Fluently: Students should circle "the World Wildlife Fund (WWF)."

p. 389 Reading Strategy: Possible response: To what other animals are pandas related? Which zoos have pandas? How can I help the pandas?

p. 389 Stop to Reflect: Possible response:
1. Giant pandas can only live in cool bamboo forests.
2. Pandas do not have many babies.

p. 390 Reading Strategy: Students should check "There are so many pandas in zoos."

p. 390 Reading Check: Possible response: Main Idea: The Chinese people and international conservation organizations are working hard to protect pandas. Supporting Detail: There are currently thirteen special panda reserves where some 800 pandas are living in safety.

p. 391 Reading Informational Materials: Authors use more than one source to get as much support for their ideas as they can and to provide varied information.

p. 392 Review and Assess

Check Your Comprehension

1. Pandas need to live in cool, damp places with plenty of bamboo.
2. Pandas eat mostly bamboo, but they also eat fish, rats, bulbs, tree bark, roots, and grasses.

Applying the Reading Strategy

3. Students might list the following questions: Why are pandas so rare? Which zoos house pandas? These questions are likely to occur to readers because they specifically relate to information in the first paragraph.
4. Students might ask the following: Who funds the reserves? Where are the reserves located? These are logical questions that relate to information in the text.

Writing Informational Materials

Possible response:
Detail: Pandas in zoos
Questions: What special environments are built for the pandas?
Where are the zoos that have pandas?
What do the pandas eat?
Sources: Web sites for different zoos
Encyclopedia
Nature or science magazines

A Christmas Carol

p. 394 Reading Literary Criticism: The criticism is written for television viewers. The subtitle "Picks & Pans: Television" indicates that it is written for television viewers.

p. 394 Read Fluently: Students should circle "But TNT's *Carol* would be worth watching if only for the lead performance of Patrick Stewart."

p. 394 Reading Strategy: The statement "Old story well told" indicates a positive response.

p. 395 Reading Literary Criticism: Possible responses: Popular actors attract audiences, so readers who recognize a favorite actor's name might watch the presentation simply to see that actor perform. The list also helps viewers to identify the characters and actors in the production.

p. 395 Read Fluently: Students should circle "Handsome, wholesome, and finely tuned, the cable web's take on Charles Dickens's 1843 masterwork is TV at its classiest."

p. 396 Reading Strategy: Students may underline any two of the following details: "there are many nifty strokes here that elevate the story above most interpretations," "peppered with sharp special effects that don't encumber the narrative, this one gets it right," and "wonderful set pieces."

p. 396 Stop to Reflect: Possible responses: Some students will say the summary is detailed enough for an understanding of the review because the nature of a review is to summarize. However, others may say the summary does not give them enough information and phrases such as "Scrooge's hum gets de-bugged" are vague and confusing.

p. 396 Reading Check: Joel Gray is Christmas Past. Desmond Barrit is Christmas Present. Tim Potter is Christmas Future.

p. 397 Reading Literary Criticism: Students should circle "The supporting actors are also first-rate."

p. 397 Reading Strategy: The critic says the strongest aspect of the performance is its "overall execution." The critic also says that Robert Halmi Sr.'s visuals are "the best so far" and that "the restrained magic is very effective."

p. 398 Reading Check: Students should circle *The Oakland Press*.

p. 398 Stop to Reflect: Students should circle the letter *b*.

p. 399 Reading Strategy: He says the set design is "enormous and gorgeous."

p. 399 Stop to Reflect: Possible response: The actors whom the reviewer mentions by name are the "standouts," or leading performers.

p. 400 Reading Strategy: Students should underline any two of the following: "debut," "in perfect keeping with Wicks's toned-down production," "not quite as charismatic a miser as Coleman," "a much darker, even scarier Scrooge," and "that much more affecting."

p. 400 Reading Informational Materials: Possible response: Such literary criticisms might be found in magazines, newspapers, books, entertainment journals, and Web sites.

p. 401 Review and Assess
Check Your Comprehension

1. The *People Weekly* critic is tired of such adaptations. The critic writes, "The Charles Dickens classic has been adapted nearly to death."

2. The Meadow Brook Theatre has produced the play many times. Readers know this because the reviewer says the theatre is "still producing" the play, and the reviewer compares the current production to past productions at the theatre.

Applying the Reading Strategy

3. Possible response: "The ex-skipper of *Star Trek: The Next Generation* . . . consistently interesting and intelligent."

4. Possible response: *People Weekly*—"So you muttered 'humbug' when you spied yet another version of *A Christmas Carol* on the TV schedule." *Variety*—"Oft-told tales are difficult to pull off. . . . " *The Oakland Press*—"Director Debra Wicks has tinkered . . . just enough to make the old holiday fruitcake seem fresh."

Writing Informational Materials

Students' paragraphs should contain comparisons and contrasts of the critics' reviews of setting, plot, characterization, and performance. The paragraphs should also explain which review best helped them to visualize the productions. Students should support their opinions with examples from the reviews.

Making Fantasy Real

p. 403 Reading Responses to Literature: The birth and death dates might be included to provide background information about the author and to provide the context of the historical period during which the author lived.

p. 403 Read Fluently: Students should circle two of the following: "Little Claus and Big Claus," "The Princess and the Pea," and "The Emperor's New Clothes."

p. 404 Reading Strategy: The writer says that in spite of the physical agony of the mermaid, the reader still feels that the prince is worth dying for.

p. 404 Reading Response to Literature: Possible response: You learn that Anderson believed that there is beauty in all creatures. The writer makes a connection between Anderson's own life and that of the swan in "The Ugly Duckling."

p. 404 Reading Informational Materials: Possible response: Some students may say that reading a response first is helpful because it provides background and context for the literary work. Others may say that a response might give away plot details and therefore spoil the fun of reading a literary work.

p. 405 Review and Assess

Check Your Comprehension

1. Anderson first published a travel diary.
2. Anderson added motivation and believability to the characters.

Applying the Reading Strategy

3. The writer believes that "The Ugly Duckling" is symbolic of Anderson's life.
4. The writer quotes a description from "The Steadfast Tin Soldier" to support her belief.

Writing Informational Materials

Students should answer each of the questions as thoroughly as possible. Their responses should show a clear understanding of the elements of a response to literature.

How to Use Your New Alarm Chronograph Timer

p. 407 Reading Directions: Studying a diagram is useful because it helps people familiarize themselves with the parts of a device before they learn how to operate it.

p. 407 Stop to Reflect: The list of features tells what functions the device is able to perform. In this case, the list of features tells you that you can use the watch to set an alarm or to time an event.

p. 407 Reading Strategy: Possible response: To begin any operation—whether setting the time or using the stopwatch—you need to be able to switch to the appropriate function, or mode.

p. 408 Reading Check: Students should circle the line "Turn to set function to ALARM."

p. 408 Reading Strategy: Possible response: The best way to explain would be to demonstrate each of the steps for setting the alarm, and then to have the person set the alarm himself or herself.

p. 408 Read Fluently: The warning beep is triggered when the set amount of time is up.

p. 409 Reading Informational Materials: You would use the boldface headings to skip to the section with the directions for the countdown timer.

p. 410 Review and Assess

Check Your Comprehension

5. You can set the timer 12 hours ahead.
6. To stop the alarm from sounding, press Button A or B.

Apply the Reading Strategy

7. The alarm chronograph timer has an analog display. It also has two buttons on the left side and a crown on the right side to control its functions.
8. Use the chronograph feature for timing someone who is running a 200-meter dash.
9. Possible response: Set the function to "Timer," and then set the desired time by pressing Button B. To start and stop the timer, press Button A. Press Button B to reset the timer.

Writing Informational Materials

Students should choose a device, and then describe how to use two separate functions in step-by-step format. For example, a student might describe how to tune in a radio station and adjust the bass level on a stereo.

Bat Attacks?

p. 412 Reading Strategy: The main point of comparison is between wooden bats and aluminum bats.

p. 412 Read Fluently: Some energy is lost when the ball compresses against the bat. The resulting friction releases energy as heat.

p. 412 Reading Strategy: Students should underline all sentences in the paragraph except the final sentence. The author's main point is that baseball players using aluminum bats hit balls farther than players using wooden bats.

p. 413 Stop to Reflect: The likely effect of professional players using aluminum bats would be more home runs. Some students might feel that more home runs would make baseball games more exciting by driving up scores. Others might feel that making home runs more common would detract from the special qualities of home runs and home run hitters.

p. 413 Reading Informational Materials: The author returns to his point that the use of aluminum bats could lead to an increase in injuries.

p. 414 Review and Assess

Check Your Comprehension

1. The author believes that aluminum bats are more dangerous because balls hit with aluminum bats tend to fly faster and farther than those hit with wooden bats. She fears the use of aluminum bats could lead to an increase in injuries.

2. Aluminum bats compress more because they are hollow inside.

Applying the Reading Strategy

3. The main point of the essay is that aluminum bats cause baseballs to fly faster and farther than wooden bats.

4. Possible responses: Many students will think the author convincingly explains why balls hit with aluminum bats travel faster and farther. Some students will dispute her point that this could lead to more injuries by pointing to the lack of evidence that this has actually taken place.

Writing Informational Materials

Students should choose a subject and write a clear, coherent essay that points out three key similarities and differences. For example, a comparison of two sports might focus on necessary skills, equipment, and physical demands on players.

Tenochtitlan: Inside the Aztec Capital

p. 416 Reading Strategy: Possible response: Heads break up the text and help you find information on specific topics. The words in a head describe what that section is about.

p. 416 Stop to Reflect: Students might say the city map is similar to modern maps because it shows streets and waterways. They might also note that the city map is different because it lacks street names and because it shows buildings and other physical qualities of the city.

p. 416 Read Fluently: Students should circle two of the following: "They built three causeways . . . to link the city with the mainland," "These were raised roads . . . supported on wooden pillars," "Parts of the causeways were bridges," "These bridges . . . prevented enemies from getting to the city," or "Fresh water was brought . . . along stone aqueducts."

p. 417 Stop to Reflect: Possible response: Tenochtitlan was a large city of one-story stone houses with flat roofs. It contained two temples on one side of the center square and the king's palace on the other side. The city was surrounded by water.

p. 417 Reading Social Studies Articles: Possible response: The Aztecs depended on corn and worshiped many gods and goddesses who were in charge of corn.

p. 418 Stop to Reflect: Possible response: The Aztecs were proficient stoneworkers and efficient architects.

p. 418 Reading Strategy: Students should underline the following: "they think it may have been between one third . . . of the population," "The rest were nobility, craftspeople, and others," "Each chinampa . . . food for one family," and "Most people . . . depended on food from outside the city."

p. 418 Read Fluently: They got their food from farms outside the city.

p. 419 Reading Strategy: 1. The rich lived in stone houses in the center of the city. The houses were washed and shone white. They were large and surrounded by courtyards that were planted with flower and vegetable gardens. 2. The poor lived on the chinampas in wattle-and-daub houses. They lived with their families in small one- or two-room huts that were part of a compound. The poor also kept turkeys in pens and beehives for honey.

p. 419 Reading Informational Materials: Most students will probably agree that this article focuses on all of the key aspects of a social studies article. The article gives information about the geographic make up of the city, life inside the city, the customs and beliefs of the people, and the structure of the family.

p. 420 Review and Assess

Check Your Comprehension

1. The city was set in the middle of a lake and swampland.
2. The wealthy lived in the center of the city. The poor lived in the outskirts on the chinampas.

Applying the Reading Strategy

3. The Aztecs used stone and wattle-and-daub.
4. The Aztecs slept on reed mats on dirt floors. They had cooking fires, but no chimneys or windows, so the houses were dark and smoky. They used clay pots and utensils and had graters, grinders, and storage containers.
5. Students should list "corn" and one of the following: tomatoes, beans, chili peppers, prickly pears, maguey cactus, and cacao.

Using Informational Materials

Possible response: 1. People might consult a social studies text to find out about a place that they would like to visit. 2. Another reason might be to learn about the political situations in other countries.

Moving Mountains

p. 422 Reading Strategy: Students should circle the word "erosion." Students should underline "The Himalayas are gradually losing mass" and "the loss of mass is affecting the Himalayas' position on Earth's surface."

p. 422 Reading Check: The Himalayas are the highest mountains in the world.

p. 422 Reading How-to Essays: A list of the materials needed for the demonstration begins under the boldface head.

p. 423 Read Fluently: Possible response: The numbering shows which step comes first and helps readers to follow the steps in the correct order.

p. 423 Reading Informational Materials: After completing the experiment, readers have the information they need to understand the effects of erosion.

p. 424 Review and Assess

Check Your Comprehension

1. Erosion is causing the Himalayas to lose their mass and shift their position on Earth.
2. Earth's crust is its rigid, outer layer that floats on a layer of molten rock.
3. The essay instructs you to do a demonstration to understand the effect of erosion.

Applying the Reading Strategy

4. Possible response: The water level will change.
5. Possible response: The experiment visually shows the causes and effects of erosion.

Writing Informational Materials

Students should give clear, step-by-step instructions, including a list of materials needed to accomplish the task.

Answers to Part 1
Unit 1

The Cat Who Thought She Was a Dog and the Dog Who Thought He Was a Cat

p. 6 Reading Strategy: Students should circle *poor farmer.*

p. 6 Vocabulary and Pronunciation: Responses will vary, depending on the students' native tongues.

p. 6 Reading Strategy: Students should circle *traveled from door to door, buying and selling things.*

peddler: someone who travels door to door, buying and selling things

p. 7 Vocabulary and Pronunciation: Students should listen to the pronunciations of native English speakers in your area and should circle "1 syllable" or "2 syllables," whichever applies.

p. 7 Vocabulary and Pronunciation:
displeased: not pleased
disbelief: the opposite of belief
disappear: the opposite of appear

p. 7 Culture Note: Responses will vary, based on student knowledge. Ask students to share their ideas.

p. 8 Vocabulary and Pronunciation: Any words students circle will depend on their native languages. For example, native Spanish speakers may circle *family*, which is similar to the Spanish *familia*, and *envied*, which is similar to the Spanish *envidiado*. Students whose native languages do not use the Roman alphabet should still consider sound-alike words with similar meanings.

p. 8 Literary Analysis: Possible response: The beauties of nature are more important than your own appearance; the world is more important than you.

p. 8 Literary Analysis: Possible response: A person's actions toward others are more important than his or her appearance; being kind and generous is more important than how you look.

Review and Assess

1. Possible response: poor, happy, loving

2. Marianna Skiba—missing tooth; first daughter—nose too snub and broad; second daughter—chin too narrow and long; third daughter—freckles; Kot—realizes she is not a dog.

3. Jan gives back the mirror because it has disrupted the house, and he realizes it is not good to spend so much time looking at one's self.

4. The following words help readers understand the meaning of the word *trinket:* jewelry and kerchiefs

5. *glimpse:* a quick look

6. Students should check the first, fourth, and fifth sentences.

Two Kinds

p. 13 Culture Note: Responses will vary, depending on the students' experiences.

p. 13 Reading Strategy: Students should circle *super, talent,* and *ed.*
Possible completed sentence: A *supertalented* child is a child with more than normal talent.

p. 13 Vocabulary and Pronunciation: Responses will vary, depending on the students' native tongues.

p. 14 Vocabulary and Pronunciation: Students should circle *when* and *why.*

p. 14 English Language Development: Students should correct the first sentence to "I only ask you to be your best" or "I only ask that you be your best." They should correct the other to "Do you think (that) I want you to be a genius?"

p. 14 Vocabulary and Pronunciation:
Students should say the word and then
write the meaning.

Possible meaning: bass: the lower sounds
of music or singing

p. 15 Reading Strategy: Students should
circle *un* and *able*.

un-: not ; *-able:* able

p. 15 Vocabulary and Pronunciation:
Students should circle *scale, cat,* and *cans*.

p. 15 Vocabulary and Pronunciation:
Students should circle the *ph*.

p. 15 English Language Development:
Students should circle *worser* and cross
out the *r* to make it *worse*.

p. 16 Culture Note: Responses will vary,
depending on the customs of students'
native lands.

p. 16 Culture Note: Responses will vary,
depending on the students' native tongues.

p. 16 Vocabulary and Pronunciation:
Students should circle *stomach*.

p. 17 English Language Development:
Students should circle *stronger*.

p. 17 English Language Development:
Students should circle both sets of
quotation marks in the mother's remarks
and both sets in Jing-mei's remarks, for a
total of eight sets of quotation marks.

The author shows a change of speaker by
indenting and sometimes also by using
explanations (dialogue tags) such as "she
shouted in Chinese" and "I shouted."

p. 17 Literary Analysis: Students should
circle *I wanted to see it spill over*.
They should also circle *anger*.

p. 18 Reading Check: Students should
number four things that Jing-mei does
that disappoint her mother: (1) She does
not get straight A's or (2) become class
president. (3) She does not get accepted to
Stanford University. (4) She even drops out
of college.

p. 18 Reading Strategy: Students should
put a line between *forgive* and *ness*.

Possible meaning: the act or state of
forgiving

p. 18 Vocabulary and Pronunciation: The
correct answer is C. Students should circle
notes and *played*.

Review and Assess

1. Students should circle *famous* and *herself*.

2. Kind 1: those who are obedient
   Kind 2: those who follow their own mind

3. She is both an obedient daughter who
   wants love and approval and an
   independent daughter who has gone her
   own way.

4. *unlike:* not similar to
   childish: like a young person
   childhood: state or condition of acting like
   a young person

5. Possible motives for pushing Jing-mei to
   be famous: hope, pride, love
   Possible motives for arranging the talent
   show: pride, competitive spirit
   Possible motives for offering the piano:
   love, forgiveness
   Possible motives for agreeing to take piano
   lessons: desire for attention, respect for
   mother, need to please mother, need to
   gain approval
   Possible motives for refusing to take more
   lessons: shame, fear, need for
   independence
   Possible motives for saying hurtful words:
   anger, shame, desire to win the battle and
   end the piano lessons

My Furthest-Back Person (The Inspiration for *Roots*)

p. 23 English Language Development: A
sixteen-year-old African; a *British-held* fort.

p. 23 Culture Note: The census just after the
Civil War was taken in 1870.

p. 23 Reading Strategy: Students might put
a line after the first comma, the second
comma, *astonishment*, the colon, the
second *Murray, well,* and *heard*. Accept
reasonable variations: for example, some
students may not put a line after *heard*.
Students should circle C, Haley's great-
grandparents.

p. 24 English Language Development:
Students should circle *didn't* and *hadn't*
and change them to *did not* and *had not*.

p. 24 English Language Development:
Students should add a *d* in each *an'* to
make *and*, a *g* in *choppin'* to make
chopping, and an *h* in *'im* to make *him*.

p. 25 Vocabulary and Pronunciation: Students should say *Kamby* with the same /a/ sound that they use for the first /a/ in *Gambia*. Most students will circle *yes*.

p. 25 Stop to Reflect: The correct answer is *D*; he said he has to get to the Gambia River, and the paragraph before said the Gambia River flows near the old kingdom of Mali in Africa.

p. 25 Reading Strategy: Students might put a line after *something, fantasized* (or after the dash), *country*, the first comma, and the second comma. Accept reasonable variations.

Students should circle *very old men* and *who could tell centuries of the histories of certain very old family clans*. Accept reasonable variations.

A *griot* is a very old African man who can tell centuries of the histories of certain very old African family clans.

p. 26 Vocabulary and Pronunciation: In this context, a *bank* is the side of a river.

Students should circle two of the following words: *upriver, left, ashore*.

p. 26 Culture Note: Kunta Kinte was about 16 years old.

p. 26 Literary Analysis: In the text, students might circle *sob, bawling*, and *weeping*.

In the margin, students should circle *joy*. Haley is proud to have made this journey and made a critical connection to his own history.

p. 27 English Language Development: Students should circle *teeth*, and write its singular form: tooth.

p. 28 English Language Development: Students' answers will vary based on their native language.

p. 28 Literary Analysis: Students should circle *cargo, choice*, and *healthy*. Also accept *Gambia, Africa*, and/or *slaves* if students can explain these answers adequately.

Review and Assess

1. Kunta Kinte was an African who was the first person in Alex Haley's family to come to America.

2. He was kidnapped near the Gambia River, shipped to Annapolis, Maryland, and sold into slavery.

3. Students should include at least five details of information.

   details of grandmother's story (African said his name was *Kin-tay*, banjo was *ko*, river was *Kamby Bolong*; *Kin-tay* chopping wood for a drum when kidnapped)—Cousin Georgia—Kansas City, Kansas

   language sounds like Mandinka; *ko* is *kora*, an old African stringed instrument; *Kamby Bolong* is likely Gambia River—Dr. Jan Vansina—Wisconsin

   Kin-tay is pronunciation of *Kinte*, clan name going back to old kingdom of Mali—Dr. Philip Curtin—Wisconsin (on phone to Dr. Vansina)

   Griots in back country tell Kinte family history; family villages of Kintes include Kinte-Kundah and Kinte-Kundah Janneh-Ya—Gambians in capital—Gambia (Africa)

   Kinte clan began in Old Mali; one member, Kairaba Kunta Kinte, settled in Juffure in Gambia; his youngest son, Omoro, wed Binta Kebba; they had 4 sons; eldest, Kunta Kinte, disappeared soon after the king's soldiers came, when he was 16 and had gone to chop wood for a drum—Kebba Kanga Fofana (griot)—Juffure, Gambia

   Col. O'Hare's Forces (British "king's soldiers") sent to James Fort in Gambia mid-1967—government records—Britain

   Lord Ligonier under Capt. Thomas Davies sailed on the Sabbath, July 5, 1767, from Gambia River to Annapolis; cargo included 3265 elephants' teeth, 800 pounds of cotton, 32 oz. Gambian gold, 140 slaves—British shipping records—Britain

   Lord Ligonier arrived in Annapolis Sept. 29, 1767; only 98 slaves survived—Annapolis Historical Society—Annapolis, Maryland

   sale of slaves from Gambia River, Africa, announced—microfilm copy of *Maryland Gazette*, Oct. 1, 1767, p. 2—Annapolis, Maryland

4. Students might draw a line after *upriver*, the first comma, *ashore*, and the second comma. Accept reasonable alternatives; for example, students might include a comma after the first *village*.

   The travelers left their boat in Albreda.

   Juffure was the village where the *griot* lived.

5. Possible responses: They are about his own family. They prove his grandmother's stories, which fascinated him as a boy. They are a source of pride to him as an African American. They reflect the origins of so many African American families. They show the pain and suffering of slavery.

A Day's Wait

p. 33 Vocabulary and Pronunciation: Students should circle *headache*.

p. 33 Vocabulary and Pronunciation: Students should circle *downstairs* and put a line between *down* and *stairs*. *Downstairs:* down the stairs; on a lower floor of the house

p. 33 Vocabulary and Pronunciation: *Advertisement:* ad; *bicycle:* bike

p. 34 English Language Development: Students should circle "past tense of *lie*, meaning 'to be resting.'"

p. 34 Culture Note: Responses will vary, depending on the students' native tongues.

p. 34 Vocabulary and Pronunciation: Responses will vary, depending on the students' native tongues. For example, Spanish speakers may list *medicina* and *médico* for *-med-*; *escribir* and *inscribir* for *-scrib-/-scrip-*; and *visibilidad* and vision for *-vid-/-vis-*.

p. 35 Literary Analysis: Students should circle *he asks whether taking the medicine will do any good* and *isn't taking it easy.*
Accept all reasonable internal conflicts. Possible response: Schatz's inner struggle seems to be between his desire to face his illness bravely and his fear and worry about what will happen to him.

p. 35 Vocabulary and Pronunciation: The correct answer is relax. Students should use the context of the conversation: *temperature is all right* and *nothing to worry about.*

p. 36 Culture Note: Answers will vary. Students should support their opinion.

Review and Assess

1. The correct answer is *C*.
2. Students' wordings will vary. On the thermometers used in France, no one can live with a temperature of 44 degrees. So

when Schatz heard the doctor say that his temperature is 102 degrees, he thinks he is sure to die.

3. Possible response: loving, patient, sympathetic, rugged

4. Schatz is (A) scared and (B) worried, BUT he tries to be (C) brave and (D) unselfish. Students may flip the order of *A* and *B* and/or the order of *C* and *D*.

    Possible examples of (A) and (B): Schatz is white faced; there are dark circles under his eyes; he is very stiff and tense; he seems detached and has trouble paying attention to his father's reading; he is evidently holding tightly onto his emotions; the next day he cries.

    Possible examples of (C) and (D): Schatz does not express his fears and holds tightly onto his emotions; he says he'd rather stay awake (i.e., to face death); even though it would be a comfort to have someone with him at this scary time, he tells father to leave because he knows it might bother the father to see his son die and orders people out of the room so that they don't catch the illness.

5. *evidently:* easily seen; clearly
    prescribed: ordered in writing; written in advance
    detached: unconnected

Was Tarzan a Three Bandage Man?

p. 41 Reading Strategy: The correct answer is *A*.
Students might circle some or all of the following: *pigeon-toed walker, walked pigeon-toed,* and *a painful form of . . .*

p. 41 English Language Development: Students should circle *fastest* and *faster*. They should label *fastest* superlative and *faster* comparative.
The comparative form compares how Robinson runs now with how he would run if he didn't walk like that.

p. 42 Culture Note: Responses will vary, depending on the popular sports in students' native lands.

p. 42 Reading Strategy: *emulate*: to admire and imitate

Students might circle [Bill and his friends] *wear a Band-Aid* and/or *the Band-Aid is just for show. . . .*

p. 42 Vocabulary and Pronunciation: Students should correct *nuthin'* to *nothing*, *kinda* to *kind of*, *coverin'* to *covering*, and *somethin'* to *something*. Some students may omit correction of kinda and coverin', the two terms already explained in the note.

p. 43 Reading Check: The correct answer is *A*.

p. 43 Reading Check: The correct answer is *B*. She will have the father make him need not a mere bandage but far more serious stitches for his wounds.

p. 43 English Language Development: Students should circle *wouldn't* (or just the *n't* part) and *no*. They might correct the sentence to "I wouldn't want to mess with a (*or* any) two-bandage man."

p. 43 Literary Analysis: Students should circle *Our hero worshipping was backwards*.

Review and Assess

1. Possible response: Bill and his friends admire the sports stars and want to be like them. Imitating the sports stars is a fad of sorts and is considered "tough" and "cool" among the boys' peers.
2. T: The mother thinks Bill's behavior is silly.
   F: The mother is a friend of Jackie Robinson's mother.

F: The mother thinks Bill's feet will fall off.
T: The mother has a good sense of humor.
F: The mother knows the names of all the popular sports heroes.

3. Suggested responses: Wearing the bandages does not really make anyone good at fighting. He is confusing the boys imitating the boxers with the actual boxers. He is confusing looking tough with being tough.
4. Suggested responses: Was the movie hero Tarzan tough and cool? Is the movie hero Tarzan worthy of imitation too?
5. Students should circle *a skin condition*.
6. *Purpose: to tell a funny, interesting story;* Possible examples: the boys imitating Jackie Robinson's pigeon-toed walk; the mother's remark, "He'd be faster if he didn't walk like that"; Bill imitating Buddy Helm's bowlegged walk; the boys wearing bandages to look like boxers; and so on.

   Purpose: to describe something important to him; Possible examples: Cosby indicating these athletes were "shining heroes" to him as a boy; showcasing his mother's wit or sense of humor; talking about what he did with his close friends of childhood (Fat Albert and the others).

   Purpose: to make a point about life or people's behavior; Possible examples: "Then, athletes were sports stars even before they started to incorporate themselves"; "Our hero worshipping was backwards."

Unit 2

In Search of Our Mother's Gardens

p. 48 Vocabulary and Pronunciation: Students should circle *sunup* and draw a line between *sun* and *up*. *Sunup* means "the time that the sun rises; sunrise; or dawn."

p. 48 Reading Strategy: Students should circle A.

p. 48 Reading Check: C.

p. 49 Culture Note: Answers will vary according to each student's country of origin. If students do not know the capital city of their native country, encourage them to use an encyclopedia or other reference source to find out.

p. 49 English Language Development: Students should circle *plainly*. *Plainly* means "clearly."

p. 50 Vocabulary and Pronunciation: Students may circle *bulbs* or *prune*. *Bulbs* commonly refers to objects used to generate electric light. (Light bulbs and planting bulbs share a similar shape.) *Prune* commonly refers to a fruit.

p. 50 Reading Strategy: Answers will vary according to each student's country of origin.

p. 51 Reading Strategy: B. *Intruded* means "interrupted." Students may say that the meaning of the root *-trud-* suggests that being intruded upon is like being pushed.

p. 51 Vocabulary and Pronunciation: Students should circle all the *l*s in *literally*.

Review and Assess

1. She thinks they owe their creative spirit to the women who have lived before them.
2. Students should check *She and her husband worked hard . . .* and *No matter how plain their house. . . .*
3. The correct answer is *B*.
4. The correct answer is *D*.
5. Students may list: her mother's perseverance in planting a garden wherever she lived; her strength in caring for it; her ability to make it beautiful; and her ability to work hard for her family.
6. *-liter-: literate*/able to read; *literacy*/ability to read.

   -nym-: synonyms/ words that mean the same thing; *antonyms*/words that have opposite meanings.

   -magni-; magnify/to enlarge; *magnificent*/large in beauty, wonder or power.

Seventh Grade

p. 56 Culture Note: Most students will say it is easier to study their native language because they begin with a stronger foundation. However, some students may note that the grammar and vocabulary of even a native language may be complex to learn.

p. 56 English Language Development: They are going to study French. He is going to visit France one day.

p. 57 English Language Development: Students should mark the dialogue as follows:

Michael: What classes . . ;
Victor: French . . . ; Michael: Spanish . . ;
Victor: I'm not . . . .

p. 57 Vocabulary and Pronunciation: Students should circle the *l* in *calmly* and pronounce the word as *KAHM lee*.

p. 57 Reading Strategy: Students may say *on the sly* means "sneakily." Students should circle catch her eye, on page 57. *Catch her eye* means "to get her attention by getting her to look at him."

p. 58 Literary Analysis: Possible response: Students may like Victor because he is trying his best, but is not able to be as smooth as he wants.

p. 58 Vocabulary and Pronunciation: *Crush* can mean to break or to reduce in size.

p. 59 Culture Note: Students should circle *wewe*. Students answers will vary based on their native language.

p. 59 English Language Development: Accept any answers that would help a students remember the spelling of the word. Some students may decide that the silent *g* in sign is like a silent stop sign.

p. 60 Stop to Reflect: Teresa might be able to help Victor in Math. Possible response: They may become friends.

p. 60 Culture Note: Students' answers will vary based on their native language.

p. 60 Vocabulary and Pronunciation: Students should circle the letter *t*.

Review and Assess

1. Victor signs up for French because Teresa was taking French, too.

   Victor is slow to leave homeroom because Teresa was still there, talking to the teacher.

   Victor goes outside during lunch because he thinks Teresa is eating outside.

   Victor pretends to know French to impress Teresa.

   Victor gets French books at the library because he wants to learn French so Teresa won't discover he does not speak the language.

2. Possible responses: Victor is embarrassed when he tries scowling. Victor is embarrassed when he says "Teresa" is a noun. Victor is embarrassed when he pretends to speak French.

3. Possible responses: Seventh grade is a time of fun, anxiety, uncertainty, or of a blooming interest in girls/boys, or of feeling self-conscious.

4. Possible responses: Amused: the incident of scowling; the boy's language when he tries to speak French. Understanding; the French teacher is kind to Victor; some of

Victor's embarrassed, self-conscious feelings.

5. *Making a face* means moving the features on your face to show an expression.

Catch her eye means "to get her attention by getting her to look."

Melting Pot

p. 65 Literary Analysis: For personal experiences, students may circle *my children* or *her mother was raised as an American.* For personal feelings, students may circle *isn't surprised.* For informal language students may circle *the parents don't speak perfect English.*

p. 65 Culture Note: Possible responses: Good point: Children will be better prepared to interact with members of the community. Bad point: Children will not have the opportunity or skills to speak with the relatives in their native country. Children will lose the chance to be bilingual.

p. 66 English Language Development: *Moneyed* probably means "wealthy."

p. 66 Vocabulary and Pronunciation: Students should circle *though* and *neighborhood.*

p. 67 Vocabulary and Pronunciation: *Panes* means sheets of glass. *Pains* means aches. Students should circle *one* and *great.*

p. 67 Stop to Reflect: Because she is "one of them."

p. 68 Reading Check: Students should mark *calamari* with *A.* Students should mark *sushi* with *B.* Students should mark *bait* with *C.*

p. 68 Reading Strategy: 1. described in a very general way; 2. a very tense place; 3. two things that don't mix easily.

p. 68 Literary Analysis: Yes, she is happy. Students should write the sentence *I am one of them, and one of us.*

Review and Assess

1. People who call America a melting pot mean that the country's values and traditions are generated by the mixing of many different groups. No one culture retains its values—instead a new set of values and traditions comes from the

mixing of cultures.

2. Students should check *It is most like a melting pot when people deal with each other person-to-person.*

3. Students should identify these conflicts: old-timers vs. young professionals; old immigrants vs. new immigrants.

4. Anna Quindlen is a young professional because she has a career and small children. She is an old-timer because she has lived in the community for a long time. She is an old immigrant because her grandparents immigrated to America.

5. *Taking over* means "taking control."

6. Possible response: Personal experience: Quindlen describes what it was like when she moved on to the block eight years earlier.

Personal feelings: Quindlen defends her neighborhood.

Informal language: half a dozen elderly men; I like you.

Humor: The antiques store used to be a butcher shop.

The Hummingbird that Lived Through Winter

p. 73 Culture Note: Possible responses: Good point: They will feel comfortable among people who share customs and language. Bad point: They may not learn the new language or customs.

p. 73 Vocabulary and Pronunciation: Students should circle *eighty.*

p. 73 Vocabulary and Pronunciation: The correct answer is *B. The dead of winter* is the time when nothing grows because it is so cold.

p. 74 Reading Check: Many students may say this is a good enough description. Others may say that the description does not include the color of the bird.

p. 74 English Language Development: The present participle of the verb *lie* is *lying.*

p. 74 Literary Analysis: Students should circle *wonderful, suspended,* and *most alive.* Student should draw boxes around *helpless* and *pathetic.* The correct answer is *D.*

p. 75 Literary Analysis: Students may circle *signs of fresh life*; the *warmth of the room; the vapor . . . ;* or *the change.*

p. 75 Reading Strategy: Students should draw a line between *rest* and *less. Restless* means without resting, or without being able to rest.

p. 76 Think Ahead: Students may predict that he will live because he is shown such care.

p. 76 English Language Development: Students may circle *swiftly* or *gently.* The adjective *swift* is changed to *swiftly* with the addition of *-ly.* The adjective *gentle* is changed to *gently* by dropping the *e* and adding *-ly. Swiftly* means "quickly." *Gently* means "with care."

Review and Assess

1. Possible responses: 1. Dikran blows warm air on the bird. 2. He feeds it honey. 3. They let the bird go.

2. Possible response: Students may say that Dikran knows it is better for a bird to be free than for it to be house bound.

3. Students should place a check before the following statements: *He can barely see; He loves and respects nature; He respects the freedom of living things.*

4. Students should place a check before the following statements. Each statement is followed by an appropriate explanation. *Hope or renewal/* He lives through winter. *The fragile or delicate nature of life:* The tiny bird could have died. The beauty and wonder of nature: *His recovery is amazing; the birds in spring are beautiful.*

5. Hummingbird: a bird that hums. Helpless: Without being able to help. Heartbreaking: Something that breaks a heart; something that is painfully sad.

Unit 3

The Third Wish

p. 81 Reading Strategy: (a) untangle. Students should circle *trying* and *entangled.*

p. 81 Culture Note: Answers may vary, but students should describe the creatures and their powers.

p. 81 Literary Analysis: Possible response: Mr. Peters expects three wishes because he knows the pattern of older fairy tales. Characters usually do not know what to expect.

p. 82 English Language Development: Students should write *elves* and *halves.*

p. 82 Reading Check: Students should circle the words *a little lonely* and *had no companion.*

p. 82 Vocabulary and Pronunciation: Students should circle the *gh* combination in *thought* and label it as *silent.* Students should also circle the *gh* combination in *laughing* and label it as *f.*

p. 82 Literary Analysis: He gets his wish. He gets a wife almost instantly.

p. 83 Stop to Reflect: Possible response: She may really be a swan.

p. 83 Literary Analysis: (d) He knows what happens in fairy tales.

p. 83 Vocabulary and Pronunciation: Students should circle *rhymes with fears.*

p. 84 Vocabulary and Pronunciation: It means clothing.

p. 84 Read Fluently: Possible response: Rhea is her swan-sister.

p. 84 English Language Development: Students should circle the question marks after the words *do you,* after *the last,* after *a swan,* and after *a girl.*

p. 85 Vocabulary and Pronunciation: Students should circle the *w* in *two.*

p. 85 Literary Analysis: Students should circle *no.* Students should circle the last sentence that describes Mr. Peters holding the withered leaf.

Review and Assess

1. He rescues a swan tangled in the weeds.

2. (b) He seems fed up with granting wishes and makes fun of human beings.

3. Possible response: His third wish was to be together in spirit with his wife. He knew she was still his companion.

4. Students should check *We are never comfortable . . . , Love sometimes means letting go . . . , What we wish for . . . and There are many different . . .*

5. In the first column students should list *three wishes; animals transforming;* and *unexpected outcomes.* In the second column students should list *a car; radio;* and *the offer of a trip around the world.*

6. (c) dark; (d) the side of a road or waterway.

The Charge of the Light Brigade

p. 90 Literary Analysis: (a) the sound of horses' hooves.

p. 90 English Language Development: Students should circle *Forward, the Light Brigade! Charge for the guns!* Quotation marks show these words are being spoken. Students should circle *A.*

p. 90 Stop to Reflect: (d) Good soldiers do not question orders.

p. 91 Reading Check: Students should answer *yes.* Students should circle *All that was left of them, Left of six hundred.*

p. 91 Vocabulary and Pronunciation: In line 30 students should label *charge* with an *n* for noun. In the title, students should also label *charge* with an *n* for noun. In line 6 students should label *charge* with a *v* for verb. In line 32 students should label *charge* with an *n* for noun.

Review and Assess

1. Students should check *They are riding . . . They are lightly armed . . . They are attacking.*

2. (a) They go forward bravely without question.

3. Many of the soldiers are killed.

4. (b) He is proud of their bravery.

5. On the first line students should write *cannon; them.* On the second line students should write *trapped.* On the third line students should write *battle.*

6. Fired on as frequently as rain drops in a storm.

The Californian's Tale

p. 96 Vocabulary and Pronunciation: Students should circle *horn* and *strike.* Students should define *horn* as *a device used to make a loud noise,* and *strike* as *to hit.*

p. 97 Literary Analysis: People were invited in and made welcome. Students should circle the last sentence of the paragraph.

p. 97 Vocabulary and Pronunciation: A stand for washing. It holds a tub or sink or container for water.

p. 98 English Language Development: Students should circle *seemed* and label it *reg.* In the next sentence students should circle *drank* and *was* and label them *irreg.*

p. 98 English Language Development: Students should circle *She'll.* Students should write the words *She will* on the line.

p. 98 Read Fluently: Possible response: He may be lonely.

p. 99 Stop to Reflect: Student should write *No.* Possible Response: He may be embarrassed.

p. 99 Vocabulary and Pronunciation: Students might circle *gaity, Henry,* and *she.*

p. 100 Literary Analysis: very; extremely.

p. 100 Vocabulary and Pronunciation: Students should circle *fiddle, banjo,* and *clarinet.*

p. 101 Literary Analysis: Students should circle *clarinet, rattling dance-music,* and *big boots.*

p. 101 English Language Development: Students should circle *gentlemen,* and write the singular form *gentleman.*

p. 101 Reading Strategy: (a) Henry lost his mind when he lost his wife, and he gets worse on the anniversary of that loss. His friends play along to try to help him get through it.

p. 102 Stop to Reflect: (d) all of the above

Review and Assess

1. (d) It is pretty and shows a woman's touch.
2. Students should write a *T* in front of *Henry talks about . . .* , *Henry lost his wife . . .* , *Henry's wife was well liked . . .* , and *Henry's wife was an educated woman . . .* Students should write an *F* in front of *Henry's wife was an orphan* and *Henry's wife knew little about . . .*
3. The miners pretend she is coming home to help Henry through this rough time of the year.
4. (a) It could be lonely but those who were there were often kind and friendly.
5. On the first line students should write *friendly; folksy.* On the second line the student should write *colorful; descriptive.* On the third line the student should write *rural; homey.* On the forth line the student should write *gathering together; playing musical instruments.*
6. Thirty-five years ago I panned for gold but I never found any.

Four Skinny Trees

p. 107 Reading Check: (a) thin and scrawny. Students should circle *skinny* and *pointy*.

p. 107 Vocabulary and Pronunciation: (a) stay; endure; refuse to give up

p. 108 Reading Strategy: (c) alone in a difficult world

Review and Assess

1. Both the speaker and the trees are skinny.
2. The speaker and the trees grow up in a poor city neighborhood.
3. Students should put a check in front of *strength, hope,* and *pride.*
4. For the first sentence students might write *Children do not belong in ghettos but often are raised there.* For the second sentence students might write *Individual strengths are often hidden.* For the third sentence students might write *Inner strength helps us reach high goals.*
5. Students should circle (a) *roots* and (b) *the trees' branches*

Unit 4

The Night the Bed Fell

p. 133 Vocabulary and Pronunciation: unhappy; unfriendly; unknown.

p. 133 Vocabulary and Pronunciation: out of your mind: not in a good state of mind; out of practice: not used to something

p. 113 Literary Analysis: Students should circle *He thinks he needs to wake up every hour. Otherwise, he might suffocate to death.*

p. 114 Reading Strategy: Students should explain why they do or do not think it is significant.

p. 114 Vocabulary and Pronunciation: Students should circle *tiptoe.*

p. 114 Reading Check: Top Floor Attic: Mr. Thurber; Next Room: James and Briggs; In Hall: Rex, the dog; Across the Hall: Roy; Floor Below Attic: Mrs. Thurber and Herman

p. 115 Reading Strategy: Students should explain what they think might happen. Yes. It is a significant event. It starts the whole chain of events.

p. 115 English Language Development: Students should circle *sniffing* and *himself.*

p. 115 Literary Analysis: Students should circle *Gugh.*

p. 116 Vocabulary and Pronunciation: Possible answers: write, wrong.

p. 116 Literary Analysis: Students should circle the following: *He thinks the house is on fire; mother thinks he is trapped under his bed; "He's dying!" . . . I'm all right!, Briggs yelled.*

p. 116 English Language Development: Students should circle *father.*

p. 116 Stop to Reflect: Students should explain why they do or do not think it is funny.

Review and Assess

1. The correct answer is (a).
2. He does these things because he is afraid he will stop breathing at night.
3. Mother: She thinks her husband is trapped under the bed. Cousin Briggs: He

thinks he is suffocating and everyone is trying to save him. Rex the Dog: He jumps on Briggs, thinking he is the culprit.

4. He probably exaggerated Briggs' fear of suffocation. The story of his Aunt Sarah leaving money for burglars outside her house might be an exaggeration. The story about his Aunt Gracie is probably an exaggeration when he says she piled shoes "about her house." The story of the dog jumping on Briggs might also be an exaggeration.

5. Students should check the following: The father goes up to the attic to sleep; Young James Thurber's cot collapses; The mother fears the attic bed fell and hurt or killed the father; Brother Herman yells to try to calm mother; Cousin Briggs pours camphor all over himself; Rex attacks Briggs; The father thinks the house is on fire and comes downstairs. Students should circle *Young James Thurber's cot collapses* as the event that causes all of the confusion.

All Summer in A Day

p. 121 English Language Development: Students should circle the question marks and put a box around the exclamation mark.

p. 121 Literary Analysis: Students should circle the following: *Venus has known nothing but rain.*

p. 121 Reading Check: They're the children of the men and women who came to Venus from Earth to set up a space colony.

p. 122 Vocabulary and Pronunciation: Possible answers: our, sour, tower, power

p. 122 Reading Strategy: Margot: quiet and shy; William: bold and mean

p. 122 English Language Development: Students should circle *drenched* and draw an arrow to *windows* from *drenched*.

p. 123 Reading Strategy: Students should circle the following contrasts: [*Margot has*] *lived on Venus for only five years. Before that, she lived on Earth./The rest of the children have lived all of their lives on Venus. She remembers the sun./Because they were only two when they saw the sun, they don't*

remember it. Possible answer: Margot's past experience might be considered a "crime" to the others because she is able to remember something they wish they could remember. They are probably jealous.

p. 123 English Language Development: die and dying.

p. 123 Reading Strategy: Students should circle the following: *Margot's parents are thinking of moving back to earth.* This probably makes the children hate her because they are jealous.

p. 123 Reading Check: Margot came to Venus five years ago, when she was four. She came from Earth.

p. 124 Reading Strategy: Students should circle the following words: *protesting, pleading,* and *crying.* The other children are mean.

p. 124 English Language Development: Not able to be believed.

p. 124 Culture Note: Students should name a similar game.

p. 125 Vocabulary and Pronunciation: calm: the *l* is silent; climb: the *m* is silent; island: the *s* is silent; overwhelm: the *h* is silent.

p. 125 Vocabulary and Pronunciation: The first *g* is soft and the second *g* is hard.

p. 126 Stop to Reflect: Students will probably say that she will feel very angry and sad.

Review and Assess

1. For seven years, it has rained constantly.

2. She is from Earth and remembers the sun; are mean to her; regret.

3. The correct answer is (b).

4. Students should check the following: Children can be mean to one another; Outsiders are often treated badly; If you are mean, you may regret it later.

5. 1. "Sometimes there were light showers; sometimes there were heavy storms; but always there was rain." 2. "She doesn't play games with the other children in the echoing tunnels of their underground city." 3. "It was the color of flaming bronze and it was very large. And the sky around it was a blazing blue tile color."

6. *Similarities:* Margot and her classmates
   1. live on Venus 2. are nine years old
   3. are eager to see the sun

   Differences: 1. Margot remembers the
   sun. Her classmates do not remember
   the sun. 2. She has been living on Venus
   for only five years. Her classmates have
   been living on Venus their entire lives.
   3. Margot did not get to see the sun
   because she was locked away in a closet.
   Her classmates went out and played in
   the sun.

The Highwayman

p. 131 Vocabulary and Pronunciation: It is
the light that shines from the moon.

p. 131 Stop to Reflect: Students should circle
(a). The details that point to the answer are
*a French cocked-hat, a bunch of lace at his
chin, a coat of claret velvet, breeches of
brown doeskin,* and *a jeweled twinkle.*

p. 132 English Language Development:
claret-velvet coat; blood-red lips.

p. 132 Literary Analysis: He's probably
jealous and dislikes the highwayman. He
might try to get the highwayman in
trouble.

p. 132 Reading Strategy: The highwayman
has probably robbed someone.

p. 133 Culture Note: Responses will vary,
depending on students' native tongues.

p. 133 Literary Analysis: Students should
circle the following: *they gag Bess and tie
her to her bed by the window. They tie a
gun called a musket to her, with the barrel
below her heart.*

p. 133 Vocabulary and Pronunciation:
knight: night; know: no; knew: new.

p. 133 Read Fluently: The correct answer is
(c).

p. 134 Literary Analysis: The following
words add to the suspense: *Nearer he
came and nearer!; Her eyes grew wide for a
moment; she drew one last deep breath.*
Students might wonder if Bess will be able
to let the highwayman know that the
soldiers are after him.

p. 134 Literary Analysis: He wants to go
back to fight the soldiers because of what
they did to Bess. Students should circle

the following: *he spurred like a madman;
with white road smoking behind him and
his rapier brandished high.*

p. 134 Reading Check: Bess shot herself
while trying to sound off a gun shot to
warn the highwayman that the soldiers
were after him.

p. 135 Reading Check: The correct answer is
(c).

Review and Assess

1. He doesn't want anyone to see him
   because he is wanted by the law.
2. Highwayman: dashing, romantic, loyal;
   Bess: beautiful, romantic, brave, loyal;
   Tim: jealous.
3. The correct answer is (d).
4. The following details help build suspense:
   1. Tied up and gagged, Bess desperately
   wants to warn her love of the danger that
   awaits him. 2. "The highwayman came
   riding/The redcoats looked to their
   priming." 3. "Nearer he came and nearer!
   Her face was like a light."
5. Tim probably told the authorities that the
   highwayman was at the inn because he is
   jealous of their love.
6. Cause: Bess pulls the trigger because she
   is trying to sound off a gun shot to warn
   the highwayman that the soldiers are
   waiting to get him. Effects: Bess kills
   herself. The highwayman hears the
   warning shot and rides away.

Amigo Brothers

p. 140 Vocabulary and Pronunciation: Jim.

p. 140 Reading Check: What: division finals;
When: seventh of August, two weeks away.

p. 140 Reading Strategy: The wall is
probably created by the tension they feel
because they have to compete against each
other.

p. 141 Vocabulary and Pronunciation: sis

p. 141 Literary Analysis: Students should
circle *Antonio nodded* and underline
Antonio.

p. 141 Reading Check: No. Students should
circle *only one of us can win.*

p. 141 Vocabulary and Pronunciation:
gotta: got to; don'tcha: don't you

p. 142 Literary Analysis: Felix: he had figured out how to psyche himself for tomorrow's fight; Antonio: Antonio was also thinking of the fight/Antonio went to sleep hearing the opening bell for the first round. The narrator is omniscient or "all knowing."

p. 142 Vocabulary and Pronunciation: affect; effect

p. 142 Vocabulary and Pronunciation: The correct answer is (b). The words *dressing gowns to match their trunks* helps explain the meaning.

p. 143 Culture Note: about 61 kilos.

p. 143 Vocabulary and Pronunciation: Students should circle *right*.

p. 143 Reading Strategy: The correct answer is (c). The words *He [Felix] missed a right cross as Antonio slipped the punch and countered with one-two-three lefts that snapped Felix's head back* help you make the inference.

p. 144 English Language Development: Students should circle *came* and *taught*.

p. 144 Vocabulary and Pronunciation: Students should circle the *ou* in *sound* and *round*.

p. 145 Reading Check: Neither boy is winning.

p. 145 Culture Note: Answers will vary.

p. 145 Reading Strategy: The correct answer is (d). Students should circle *No matter what the decision, they knew they would always be champions to each other.*

p. 145 Reading Check: The announcer points to no one as the winner because the boys have already left the ring, arm in arm.

Review and Assess

1. The correct answer is (b).
2. How it brings them together: they worked out together and went running together. How it drives them apart: They have to compete against each other, and only one person can win.
3. Tall-A; short—F; dark—F; fair—A; boxes better when he comes in close—F; boxes more gracefully—A; has better moves as a boxer—F; keeps boring down on his opponent—F
4. Friendship is more important than winning.
5. Felix: 1. Felix knew they could not "pull their punches," or hold back when they fought 2. he had figured out how to psyche himself
   Referee: The referee was stunned by their savagery.
   Crowd: The fear soon gave way . . .
6. Antonio and Felix work very hard to fulfill their dreams about boxing; The Golden Gloves is an important tournament in the world of boxing.

Unit 5

Our Finest Hour

p. 151 Reading Check: Students should circle the following words: *means sitting there in the studio and telling some stories into the camera and introducing the reports and pieces that other reporters do.* Students should circle (a) the main announcer.

p. 152 Vocabulary and Pronunciation: Students should circle *second time*.

p. 152 Literary Analysis: They thought they had fixed the problem, but they had not. A political story from Washington, D. C. was supposed to be introduced, but pictures of people in France pretending to be dead to show the dangers of smoking came up on the monitor.

p. 152 English Language Development: 1. had seen 2. decided 3. come

p. 153 Literary Analysis: Students should circle the following: *French people pretending to be dead* and *myself, bewilderment and all.* The fact that he sees himself is funny because he's feeling bewildered by what is happening, he doesn't realize they are coming back to him, and then he sees himself with a look of bewilderment on his face.

p. 153 Vocabulary and Pronunciation: Students should circle (b).

p. 153 Vocabulary and Pronunciation: The practice of reporting.

Review and Assess

1. Students should circle answer (d).

2. Students should circle *calm* and *professional.*

3. No. His words are a follow-up to the fill-in producer yelling "What is going on?" so he was probably having fun with what had happened.

4. **Supposed to Happen:** He introduced his first report. **Actually Happened:** He saw himself on the monitor and then a different story was introduced. **Supposed to Happen:** He introduced a political story from Washington, D. C. **Actually Happened:** Pictures of people in France pretending to be dead to show the dangers of smoking came up on the monitor. **Supposed to Happen:** Osgood introduced a story about rafting. **Actually Happened:** Nothing happened on the monitor.

5. Any of the following details show that the author's purpose is mainly to entertain:

   • Osgood starts by explaining that he introduced his first report and then builds to make his point that a story came on that was not the story he introduced.

   • Then, Osgood explains that a political story from Washington, D.C. was supposed to be introduced, but pictures of people in France pretending to be dead to show the dangers of smoking came up on the monitor.

   • He explains how the monitor shows him with a bewildered look on his face.

   • He tells us how the fill-in producer screamed so loud "half of America" could hear him.

   • He ends his story by telling us the humorous way that the head of CBS responded to the incident.

Cat on the Go

p. 158 Culture Note: sittin' = sitting; 'e = he; 'im = him

p. 158 Literary Analysis: Students should circle the following: *I went home for a blanket and brought 'im round to you.*

p. 158 Vocabulary and Pronunciation: "WOONd" and "injury" are used here.

p. 158 Reading Strategy: Students should circle answer (b).The words *terrible wound* show us that the cat is very badly hurt. The words *There's nothing anybody can do about . . . about that* also show us that it seems like a hopeless situation for the cat.

p. 159 Think Ahead: Some students may think he will survive because his purrs are a positive sign.

p. 159 Reading Strategy: Students should circle (a) try.

p. 159 Stop to Reflect: He needs to sit still so that he can rest and heal.

p. 159 Reading Check: The correct answer is (b).

p. 160 Literary Analysis: He is playful and friendly.

p. 160 English Language Development: Students should circle *Mothers'* and label it *pl* for *plural.*

p. 160 Literary Analysis: Students should circle *seemed to enjoy himself, enjoyed the slides,* and *was very interested in the cakes.*

p. 161 English Language Development: Students should circle *getting* in the sentence *He likes getting around. . . .*

p. 161 Vocabulary and Pronunciation: Students should circle *ue.* The following words rhyme with tongue: hung, lung, rung, and sung.

p. 161 Literary Analysis: Possible answer: considerate and generous.

p. 162 Vocabulary and Pronunciaton: Students should circle *ah* and *'im.* ah = I; 'im = him.

p. 162 Vocabulary and Pronunciaton Students should circle these words and label as follows: walked-R, opened-R, strode-I, took-I, leaped-R; put-I, stroked-R

Review and Assess

1. The correct answer is (c).

2. He purrs after being seriously injured. He likes to be a cat-about-town.

3. The Herriots are very sad about returning Oscar, but they also realize that he should be with his original owners because they had him first and they love him very much.

4. The correct answer is (b).

5. Oscar the Cat: friendly and affectionate; James Herriot: skilled as a doctor and a good storyteller; Helen Herriot: caring

6. Oscar was always visiting people and places. Let's try this. The two boys screamed with excitement.

The Luckiest Time of All

p. 167 Vocabulary and Pronunciation: It used to be a show that traveled throughout the south.

p. 167 Reading Strategy: Students should circle the following text: *somethin like the circus.*

p. 167 Culture Note: She probably calls her "Sweet Tee" as a loving term to show that she is precious and dear to her.

p. 168 English Language Development: Ovella and I walked through every place we had walked through before.

p. 168 Vocabulary and Development: Elzie did not want to lose her lucky stone. When the dog was loose, it chased Elzie.

p. 169 Read Fluently: Elzie says she is luckier than anybody for meeting her husband, but then in the last sentences she says that *most* of the time she thinks she's lucky. There are probably times when she's frustrated with her husband, so she's being funny when she says "Least mostly I think it."

Review and Assess

1. Students should circle two of the following words: adventurous, fun-loving, and shy. Adventurous: they want to join Silas Greene to see the world. Fun-loving: They want to join in on the excitement when they see the dancing dog and people throwing money for the dog. Shy: Elzie says she felt shy when she walked toward Amos.

2. Students should circle the following words: heroic, thoughtful, protective, nice.

3. It was unlucky because it hit the dog's nose and the dog chased her. It's lucky because the dog-chase led to her meeting her husband.

4. One example is when she calls the dog the "cutest one thing in the world next to you." Another example is when she refers to Amos as the "finest fast runnin hero in . . . Virginia." Another example is when she says the dog "lit out after me and I flew."

5. After all those years, she can look back and see how important that funny experience was in her life. She can realize how different life probably would have been for her if she had not had that experience. Certain moments probably stand out in her mind more than other moments, so her use of hyperbole helps stress those particular moments and add more excitement to her story.

6. (c) spotted; (b) holding gently

How the Snake Got Poison

p. 174 English Language Development: Students should circle *suit (verb): to go well with.*

p. 174 Read Fluently: Students should circle *Ah* for *I* and *de* for *the.*

p. 174 Culture Note: The following are the dialect words and their meanings: Ah=I, nothin'=nothing, stompin'=stomping, lak=like, dat=that, dis=this, yo'=your, mouf=mouth, tromps= tramp, yo'self=yourself.

p. 175 Literary Analysis: The snake feels he needs protection so he won't be stomped on and so that his generation won't be killed off, but the small animals feel they need protection from the snake so he won't kill them and their generations.

p. 175 Vocabulary and Pronunciation: The correct answer is (b) We're scared.

p. 175 Reading Strategy: Students should circle (b). Students should explain why they agree or disagree.

Review and Assess

1. God gives the snake poison so that he'll be protected and so that his generation won't be killed off.

2. The correct answer is (c) by warning friends.

3. The story couldn't end that way because in reality snakes are poisonous and have rattles.

4. The small animals complain that the snake's poison is killing their generations. The snake explains that he has to protect himself because all he sees is feet coming to step on him and he can't tell who is his enemy and who is his friend.

5. Students should check the following: *A snake's rattles protect small animals from the snake; All types of animals created by God deserve to remain on earth; Animals have special traits or abilities to help them survive.*

Unit 6

Rikki-tikki-tavi

p. 180 Reading Check: Students should circle *a small furry animal that kills snakes.* The word *bungalow* is also explained in this paragraph. Students should put a box around the word *bungalow* and circle the words *one-story house.*

p. 180 English Language Development: Students should circle *he revived* to indicate that the mongoose was in the process of waking up.

p. 180 Vocabulary and Pronunciation: Students should write *generosity; liberality in giving*

p. 181 English Language Development: Students should circle adjective: not friendly, unkind.

p. 181 Literary Analysis: (b) rising action

p. 182 Reading Strategy: Rikki thinks he will fight Nag later.

p. 182 Reading Check: Students should circle *It must be the head.* Possible response: Yes, because Rikki is a born snake killer.

p. 183 Vocabulary and Pronunciation: Students should circle *up and down; round in great circles; shaken to pieces; behind him*

p. 183 Vocabulary and Pronunciation: Students should circle *bang-stick.* The term is appropriate because it accurately describes what a shotgun looks like and sounds like.

p. 183 Reading Strategy: (a) try to kill Nagaina. Even with Nag dead, Nagaina is still a danger.

p. 184 Vocabulary and Pronunciation: (b) able to reach out and bite easily

p. 184 English Language Development: Students should circle *Look at your friends; Look at your eggs; Go and look; Give it to me.* Students should write *you* before each command.

p 185 Literary Analysis: Nagaina is killed by Rikki. Killing the last villain helps fix the problem.

p. 185 English Language Development: Students should write *knives; leaves; wolves; beliefs.*

Review and Assess

1. Students should circle *brave, nosey.*

2. Mongooses are born to kill snakes; Rikki wants to protect Teddy from the cobra.

3. (d) He wants to clear the garden of deadly cobras.

4. 1. Nag eats a baby bird. 2. Nagaina sneaking up behind Rikki to do him harm. 3. Karait striking at Rikki.

5. The climax is when Nag is killed.

6. Students should write *We learn that Rikki is a natural predator of snakes; Rikki hears Nagaina mention the eggs are soon to hatch; Nagaina snuck up behind Rikki.*

After Twenty Years

p. 190 Vocabulary and Pronunciation: (c) a regular path or round that a person makes

p. 190 Reading Strategy: Students should circle *the man* and *spoke.* Students should then use lines to separate the beginning and end of the sentence.

p. 190 English Language Development: Students should circle the double quotation marks before *Until* and *It*, and after *ago* and *then.* Students should circle the single quotation marks before *Big* and after *Joe.*

p. 191 Vocabulary and Pronunciation: Students should write *18; 20; 20; 20.*

p. 191 Vocabulary and Pronunciation: (a) absolutely; yes indeed

p. 191 Reading Check: Students should circle *I've had to compete with some of the sharpest wits going to get my pile . . .*

p. 192 Literary Analysis: Students should circle *with collar turned up to his ears*. This may mean the man is not Jimmy Wells.

p. 192 Stop to Reflect: (c) Both a and b seem likely.

p. 193 Literary Analysis: Most students will be surprised by this ending. The ending makes sense because it allows Jimmy to do his duty by having Bob arrested, while not making himself arrest his old friend.

Review and Assess

1. Bob and Jimmy agreed to meet at a specific time and place.
2. (b) They were close in childhood but have taken different paths in life.
3. Students should check *He wants to keep a promise . . . , He wants to show off . . . , He is curious . . .*
4. Jimmy is unable to arrest Bob himself because of the friendship and bond they once had.
5. Jimmy recognizes Bob as a criminal, the reader learns that Jimmy is the police officer, and Jimmy has another officer pose as himself to arrest Bob.
6. The police officer knows about the restaurant and when it was torn down; The police officer is probing Bob for details of his success out west.
7. Students should circle *a man leaned*. Students should draw lines between *store* and *a*, and between *leaned* and *with*. The man leaned in the doorway of a darkened hardware store. An unlit cigar was in his mouth.

Papa's Parrot

p. 198 Stop to Reflect: Students should circle *Though* and *merely*. (b) Harry's

p. 198 Vocabulary and Pronunciation: (a) visitors; companionship

p. 199 Literary Analysis: Students should circle *embarrassed* and label it *D*. Students should circle *he keeps* and label it *I*.

p. 199 Vocabulary and Pronunciation: Students will have varying answers.

p. 199 Reading Check: Students should circle all words in quotation marks. Students should label *H* any phrase followed by *Harry said* or *Harry mumbled*. Students should label the other circled words *R*.

p. 200 Reading Fluently: (a) annoyed

p. 200 Stop to Reflect: His father

Review and Assess

1. Students should check *He has outgrown the store . . . , He and his friends now . . . , He is embarrassed . . .*
2. (d)
3. Harry learns that his father is lonely and misses him.
4. Students should write *Harry Tillian liked his papa*. Students should write *Mr. Tillian looked forward to seeing his son*.
5. Students should write *he keeps walking*. Students should write *Harry had always stopped in to see his father at work*.
6. Students should write *yes* or *no* and explain their responses.

Ribbons

p. 205 English Language Development: Students should circle the exclamation marks.

p. 205 Reading Check: Students should circle *Chinese for grandmother*. Students should write *mother*

p. 205 Reading Strategy: Students should circle *What's wrong with her feet?* Students might ask *Why is she sensitive?*

p. 206 Vocabulary and Pronunciation: Students should circle one *l* and *t*.

p. 206 Reading Check: Ballet Lessons; her room

p. 206 English Language Development: Students should circle *had brought; have bought; will have caught*.

p. 207 Literary Analysis: Students should circle *Grandmother is a hero*.

p. 207 Reading Check: Students should circle *grandmother; mom; daughter*.

p. 207 Vocabulary and Pronunciation: Students should read the words aloud.

p. 207 English Language Development: Students should circle *dropped*.

p. 208 Think Ahead: That something is wrong with Grandmother's feet.

p. 208 Reading Strategy: Students should circle *What happened to your feet?* Students might ask *Was that very painful?*

p. 208 Literary Analysis: (a) People try to spare their loved ones from pain.

p. 209 Literary Analysis: Students should check *People will undergo . . . , People will do painful things . . .*

p. 209 Vocabulary and Pronunciation: Students should circle *children*.

p. 209 Stop to Reflect: The invisible ribbon is a bond between the women.

Review and Assess

1. Students should check *Grandmother is a brave woman . . . , Grandmother values freedom . . .*

2. (d) She can talk more with Ian, who has learned more Chinese.

3. Grandmother thinks the ribbons are for binding Stacy's feet.

4. (d) the loving family ties between Stacy, her mother, and Grandmother.

5. Students should check *Love and understanding . . . , We don't want those we love . . . , The best way to know a person . . .*

6. Students may ask questions such as *Why is grandmother so secretive? Because she is trying to shield her granddaughter. Why does grandmother treat Stacy differently than Ian? Because that is Chinese culture. What did grandmother's feet look like? Deformed.*

The Treasure of Lemon Brown

p. 214 Vocabulary and Pronunciation: 1. team 2. teem 3. principal 4. principle

p. 214 Reading Check: Students should circle *dark* or *angry*.

p. 214 Vocabulary and Pronunciation: (b) to read steadily and often

p. 215 Stop to Reflect: Students may say that Greg's father was trying to encourage Greg to work hard.

p. 215 Vocabulary and Pronunciation: Students should circle *For a moment; listened carefully but it was gone; as soon as the rain let up; about to look*

p. 215 Reading Strategy: Students will have varying questions.

p. 216 English Language Development: Students should write *Do you not have a home? Are you after my treasure? As I said, I have a razor. What do you mean, if I have one? Every man has a treasure. If you don't know that you are foolish.*

p. 216 Reading Strategy: Students will have varying questions.

p. 216 Vocabulary and Pronunciation: Students should circle *flashlight* and *wallpaper*. Students should write *A flashlight is a small portable light that illuminates in a flash. Wallpaper is decorated paper that covers a wall.*

p. 217 Vocabulary and Pronunciation: Students should circle the *e* in *He*, the *ee* and *ie* in *eerie*, the *e* in *Maybe*, the first *e* in *scene*, the *e* in *be*, the first *e* in *even*, and the *ee* and *i* in *eerier*.

p. 217 Read Fluently: (c) proud

p. 217 Literary Analysis: Students should circle *Brown felt like his son would be able to do something if he knew his father had.* (c) Greg's father telling how he studied hard to pass the postal test.

p. 218 English Language Development: Students should insert the word *Of* before the word *'Course*.

p. 218 Stop to Reflect: Lemon's experiences may allow Greg to realize the accomplishments of his father and will bring Greg and his dad closer together.

p. 218 English Language Development: Students should change *foolishest* to *most foolish*.

p. 219 Stop to Reflect: Possible response: Greg smiles because he can now appreciate his father's lecture. He is looking forward to listening to his father.

Review and Assess

1. (d) He is blocks from home, and the rain is very heavy.

2. (c) They have heard that Brown has a treasure and want to steal it.

3. poor: homeless/lives in empty old building; dresses in rags

   talented: got good reviews for playing harmonica and singing blues

   loved family: traveled all over, working hard, to support his wife and son

   proud: gave clippings of reviews of his performances to his son

   sad: grieves for loss of wife and son

4. his old harmonica and clippings of old reviews of his performances

5. Students should put a check in front of *A person's achievements are a treasure that can be passed down* and *Just about everyone has a treasure of some kind.*

6. Possible question: What is Lemon Brown's treasure? Answer: an old harmonica he used to play when he performed, and clippings of old reviews of his performances

   Possible question: Why does the treasure have special meaning to him? Answer: He gave it to his son, who treasured it and had it with him when he was killed in the war.

   Possible question: What does Greg learn from Lemon Brown? Answer: to value his father's proud achievements and concern for Greg

Unit 7

I Am a Native of North America

p. 224 Culture Note: White Society differs from Native Americans in that it values material possessions. The societies are similar in that they both enjoy social gatherings.

p. 224 Reading Check: People learned to live with one another; learned to serve one another; learned to respect the rights of one another.

p. 224 Reading Strategy: Students should circle *nature was considered a gift and treat nature well.*

p. 225 Reading Strategy: Students should circle *They stripped the land and poisoned the water and air.*

p. 225 English Language Development: Students should circle *lowest* and *greatest*.

p. 225 Literary Analysis: Without love we become weak.

p. 226 Vocabulary and Pronunciation: (c) physical

p. 226 Reading Strategy: Students should write *Many young people have forgotten the old ways. They have been made to feel ashamed of their Indian ways.*

p. 226 Reading Check: Native Americans must forgive the terrible sufferings the white society brought.

Review and Assess

1. Native American and White Society

2. Native Americans view nature as a gift that should be respected.

3. The author's idea of brotherhood is love and forgiveness.

4. Under *Native American Culture* students should write *People learn to respect the rights of their neighbors through communal living; People love and respect nature.* Under *White Society* students should write *People live near one another but do not know or care about their neighbors; People abuse nature.*

5. The author provided support for his main idea by explaining how well the Native American culture lived. He compares how the Native Americans used their natural resources to how the white society abused them.

All Together Now

p. 231 Vocabulary and Pronunciation: (c) The major groups into which human beings are divided based on physical features.

p. 231 Reading Check: No. People bring peace between races, not laws.

p. 231 Literary Analysis: Students should underline *Each of us can decide to have one friend of a different race or background.*

p. 232 English Language Development: Students should underline *One thing is clear . . . their inner reality.*

p. 232 Reading Strategy: Students should underline *Babies come into the world as blank as slates* and *Children learn ideas and attitudes from the adults*

p. 232 Literary Analysis: Students should circle *Parents can actively encourage their children to be in the company of people who are of other racial and ethnic backgrounds.*

Review and Assess

1. people
2. Civil Rights Act of 1964; Voting Rights Act of 1965. Laws cannot create tolerance; people's attitudes have to change.
3. The author means babies are innocent and can be taught anything by their parents and teachers.
4. The author is dedicated to bringing people together. She wants people to work towards racial peace.
5. Possible response: Do the supporting details make sense? Do they persuade me to accept the author's point of view? Students' responses to the second question may vary, but they should explain their answers.

How to Enjoy Poetry

p. 237 Literary Analysis: Students should underline *When you really feel it, a new part of you happens, or an old part is renewed, with surprise and delight at being what it is.*

p. 237 English Language Development: Students should underline *go together* and *some go.*

p. 237 Vocabulary and Pronunciation: *Deep* means to explore something in a serious way, focusing on things that are not easily noticed.

p. 238 Reading Strategy: Students should underline *Poetry can describe the sun and stars in different ways and from different perspectives.*

p. 238 Literary Analysis: Dickey explains how to begin writing poetry.

p. 238 Reading Check: The writer says you need to begin with yourself to start enjoying poetry.

p. 239 English Language Development: Students should circle *more memorable*

p. 239 Stop to Reflect: Yes. Both reading and writing poetry help you to look at your own life differently. Reading and writing poetry help you make connections between things that you have never connected before.

Review and Assess

1. (c) poetry comes to you from outside you and something from within you must meet it
2. Giving to poetry means allowing yourself to get into the words and feel their meanings.
3. Rhythm and rhyme are important to poetry because they make the words more memorable and more pleasant to read.
4. Dickey explains that poetry can uncover a new part of you, and he explains how poetry comes to you from the outside.
5. 1. When you really feel poetry, a new part of you happens. 2. To understand poetry is to know it comes to you from outside. 3. You must make a gut connection with the poetry.

from An American Childhood

p. 244 English Language Development: Students should circle *thought.*

p. 244 Culture Note: Students' responses will vary.

p. 244 Vocabulary and Pronunciation: Students should circle *waited for cars* and *with snowballs.* Students should write *the meaning of pelted is to be hit with something thrown.*

p. 245 Reading Strategy: Students should circle *He was in city clothes: a suit and tie, street shoes.* The purpose for including this information is to describe the challenge this driver took on when he decided to chase the kids in the snow.

p. 245 English Language Development: Students should circle *across, over, up, through, between*

p. 245 Stop to Reflect: Students answers will vary.

p. 246 Literary Analysis: Dillard's description of the events tells us she enjoys challenges and seeks excitement.

p. 246 Reading Strategy: Dillard wants to show the level of difficulty and the toll the chase has taken on the pursuer.

p. 246 English Language Development: (b) calmed down and came back to reality. Dillard means the man began to start thinking clearly.

p. 247 Reading Check: Dillard feels the most satisfying thing about her experience is that she went all out and did her very best in a challenging situation.

Review and Assess

1. Dillard enjoys the competition and mental and physical aspects of football.
2. Dillard is outgoing. Dillard is competitive.

3. Dillard feels the man was a worthy opponent. She tells us this by describing how difficult the chase was for everyone involved.
4. A passage that entertains: *He ran after us, and we ran away . . . we were running for our lives.* A passage that teaches a lesson: *Then she realized that the man knew the same thing she did: You have to throw yourself into an activity with all your energy if you want to win.* A passage that explains something about the author: *Your fate. . . . Nothing girls did could compare to it.*

Unit 8

A Christmas Carol: Scrooge and Marley, Act 1, Scenes 1 & 2

p. 252 Reading Strategy: Students should respond with their own ideas of what a ghost looks like.

p. 252 Vocabulary and Pronunciation: (b) joke

p. 253 Vocabulary and Pronunciation: A poulterer sells poultry.

p. 253 Reading Check: The story takes place on Christmas Eve, 1843.

p. 253 Vocabulary and Pronunciation: (b) spending money only when necessary

p. 254 Reading Strategy: Students should circle *ancient, awful, dead-eyed*

p. 254 English Language Development: Students should underline *asking*

p. 254 Reading Check: He doesn't think his nephew should be merry because he is poor.

p. 254 Vocabulary and Pronunciation: Students should circle *dismal.*

p. 255 Literary Analysis: Bah! Humbug!

p. 255 English Language Development: Students should circle all the exclamation marks in the passage and then read the passage with emotion and excitement.

p. 255 Vocabulary and Pronunciation: Students should circle *family, refuses, after*

p. 256 English Language Development: It is six o'clock, so the clock rings six times.

p. 256 Literary Analysis: Students should circle *Cratchit smiles faintly.*

p. 256 Reading Check: Cratchit gets one day off a year.

p. 256 Reading Check: Cratchit wants to say Merry Christmas. Scrooge hates Christmas.

p. 257 Reading Strategy: The scenery changes from an office to a street scene. Music is heard. People walk by.

p. 257 Literary Analysis: Scrooge is grumpy and snaps at passing boys. The other characters are happy and cheerful.

Review and Assess

1. Jacob Marley is Scrooge's former business partner. He is a ghost in this play.
2. Scenes 1 and 2 take place in Scrooge's place of business, a countinghouse.
3. Scrooge is stingy and he doesn't want to pay Cratchit for a day when he doesn't work.
4. *Things Scrooge Says:*

   Bah! Humbug!

   Every idiot who goes about with "Merry Christmas" on his lips, should be boiled with his own pudding, and buried with a stake of holly through his heart.

   Things Scrooge Does:

   He refuses to go to his nephew's for Christmas dinner.

   He refuses to give the kind men a donation for the poor.
5. Reading Strategy:
   - How he moves: Possible response: He walks slowly, with a cane. He is bent over.

- His facial expressions: Possible response: He frowns. He says mean things under his breath. He tries to hit people with his cane.

A Christmas Carol: Scrooge and Marley, Act 1, Scenes 3–5

p. 262 Vocabulary and Pronunciation: When something disappears, it goes out of view or existence.

p. 262 Reading Check: He sees Jacob Marley's face on the door knocker.

p. 262 Reading Strategy: Students should circle *horrible to look at, pigtail, vest, suit as usual, drags an enormous chain, is transparent*

p. 263 Literary Analysis: Students should draw a sketch of the scene as it is described.

p. 263 Culture Note: Students should tell what the names of the coins and bills are in their country.

p. 263 Reading Check: He screams a ghostly scream and takes off his head.

p. 263 Stop to Reflect: He did not care for other people during his life. All he cared about was money.

p. 263 Reading Strategy: Students should use their imaginations to picture this figure. Possible response: A child with the head of an old man.

p. 264 Vocabulary and Pronunciation: Students should circle *do, through*

p. 264 Literary Analysis: Students should circle *panicked*

p. 264 English Language Development: Students should circle *open, soft, downy, country. Open* follows a linking verb.

p. 265 English Language Development: Students should circle *crying, singing, weeping, dancing, playing*

p. 265 Reading Check: Students should underline *he thinks of the young caroler whom he shooed away from his office earlier that night. He says he wishes he had given him something.*

p. 265 Reading Check: He thinks about Cratchit. He wishes that he had been kinder to him.

p. 265 Reading Strategy: They describe how the boy Ebenezer is replaced by a man Ebenezer. The co-workers disappear and a young woman in mourning clothes appears.

p. 266 Reading Check: money.

p. 266 Reading Check: The world is hard on people who are poor and it punishes people who try to be rich.

p. 266 English Language Development: Students should circle *nobler, wiser*

p. 267 Reading Check: She is releasing him from marrying her.

p. 267 Vocabulary and Pronunciation: Students should circle *ch* and *tu*

p. 267 Reading Check: The ghost of Christmas Past appears, Scrooge sees himself as a lonely boy in the schoolhouse. Scrooge sees his former boss and coworkers. Scrooge sees himself and a woman.

Review and Assess

1. Marley's ghost has to carry the chain because he didn't care for other people in life.

2. The Ghost of Christmas Past visits Scrooge after Marley leaves.

3. Scrooge as a young boy: Scrooge cries.
   Scrooge as a twelve-year-old boy: He says he loved his sister.
   Scrooge with his coworkers: He wishes he had been kinder to Cratchit.
   Scrooge with his fiancée: He yells "No!"

4. Scrooge was a lonely boy. Scrooge had a sister whom he loved. Scrooge was engaged at one time.

5. He panics.

Unit 9

The Cremation of Sam McGee

p. 272 Reading Strategy: Students should underline *it stabbed like a driven nail*. The cold air is being compared to a driven nail as it stabs through the parka into the body.

p. 272 Reading Check: Sam McGee was miserable because he was from the south and wasn't used to cold weather.

p. 272 Reading Strategy: Students should circle *chilled clean through to the bone*.

p. 272 Reading Check: Last remains refers to a dead body.

p. 273 Literary Analysis: Sam dies from the cold.

p. Stop to Reflect: Possible response: The fire may warm Sam back to life.

p. 274 Literary Analysis: Students should check *Character*, *Setting*, and *Plot*. Sam the *character* is speaking, the cold *setting* is described, and the plot is covered by Sam speaking and the narration.

Review and Assess

1. unbearably cold
2. He is trying to earn money.
3. He promises to cremate Sam's body.
4. Sam felt so bad, the narrator felt obligated to keep his promise.
5. Sam McGee sitting up getting warm.
6. 1. setting: The cold Arctic. 2. characters: Sam McGee. 3. rhythm: Well he seemed so low that I couldn't say no.
7. Students should complete the *What it means* part with *it was unbearably cold; a very bright smile;* and *I tried not to be afraid*.

Annabel Lee

p. 279 Reading Check: She died from the cold.

p. 279 Literary Analysis: Students should circle *me, sea, chilling, killing*, and *Lee*.

p. 279 English Language Development: Students should circle *older than* and *wiser than*.

p. 279 Literary Analysis: Students should read the bracketed lines aloud putting emphasis on the underlined words.

p. 280 Reading Strategy: Every night I lay down by my wife's grave.

p. 280 Stop to Reflect: 1. Lonely. 2. Angry. 3. Bitter

Review and Assess

1. The narrator blames the angels and the cold for Annabel Lee's death. The narrator believes the angels were jealous of the love between him and Annabel.
2. The narrator talks about the sea because the young lovers lived near the sea.
3. Students should underline *love, stronger far, love those, older, we, many, wiser*, and *we*
4. Students should list *beams/dreams*, and *rise/eyes*, *sea/Lee* and *nighttide/bride/side* as the sets of rhyming words in the final stanza.
5. The moon and stars remind me of Annabel Lee.

Maestro

p. 285 Vocabulary and Pronunciation: *Bow* means to bend forward at the waist. Students should circle the word *bow* in line 16.

p. 285 Reading Strategy: *Upturned* means to be facing upwards. Students should write the words *turned up*.

p. 285 Stop to Reflect: A song can be sung so beautifully that one might describe it as tasting great rather than sounding great. *Sweet on the tongue* is an example of this.

Review and Assess

1. The voice, the guitar, and the violin.
2. Sentimental, happy, proud.
3. Students should circle the word *strummed*.
4. Under *Clues that help Clarify*, students should write *in the air; to snare*. Beneath *Clarified Meaning*, students should write *to be tossed up in the air*.

The Village Blacksmith

p. 290 Literary Analysis: Students should circle *his brawny arms are strong as iron bands.* This comparison tells us that the blacksmith has great strength.

p. 290 Reading Strategy: Students should circle the words *he hears the parson pray and preach, he hears his daughter's voice.*

p. 290 Reading Check: The blacksmith cries because he is remembering his wife who has passed away.

p. 291 Vocabulary and Pronunciation: Students should replace *thee* and *thou* with *you.*

Review and Assess

1. The blacksmith's life is difficult. His daily work involves dealing with extreme heat and lifting heavy materials.
2. Rough; large; strong.
3. His daughter singing reminds the blacksmith of his dead wife.
4. The correct answer is a furnace.
5. In the spaces under *Sense*, students should write *Sight; Touch; Sound.* In the spaces under *Sensory Language*, students should write *Spreading chestnut tree; Strong as iron hands; He hears the parson pray and preach.*

Unit 10

Popocatepetl and Ixtlaccihuatl

p. 296 Background: Answers will vary.

p. 296 English Language Development: Students should circle *on occasion.*

p. 297 Reading Strategy: Students should read ahead to see if the Emperor makes wise decisions.

p. 297 Reading Check: Students should underline *forbade her to marry.*

p. 297 Vocabulary and Pronunciation: Students should circle *rule.*

p. 297 Reading Check: The Emperor trusted no one.

p. 298 Reading Strategy: Answers will vary. The Emperor must have had wisdom to rule for so long. The Emperor never had wisdom if he forbade his daughter to marry.

p. 298 Vocabulary and Pronunciation: Students should say the word *success.* Students should circle *Mexico.*

p. 298 Reading Check: As a reward, the emperor offers the hand of his daughter and the equal right to reign and rule Tenochtitlan.

p. 298 Literary Analysis: Aztecs regarded warriors as heroes and war as a battle for honor.

p. 298 Reading Check: The warriors report false news because they were jealous of Popo's success.

p. 299 Reading Check: Ixtla dies because she believes her love has been killed in battle.

p. 299 Reading Strategy: Student should read ahead to find details about Popo that make him more than an ordinary man.

p. 299 Literary Analysis: The warriors could not have built the pyramid in one day. This is part of the folk tale that makes it sound miraculous.

p. 299 Reading Check: Popo buries Ixtla's body at the top of the pyramid.

p. 300 Literary Analysis: Students should check *Popo had two pyramids . . . , Popo stood next to Ixtla's . . .*

p. 300 Stop to Reflect: No. This is an Aztec folk tale that was written as a fictional account of the mountains' origins.

Review and Assess

1. The emperor forbids them to marry.
2. By offering his daughter as a reward, he does not recognize her wishes.
3. Students should circle (a) The kingdom ends up with no ruler.
4. Ixtla dies because she believes the man she loves has been killed in battle.
5. Reading ahead sometimes helps you better understand what is happening earlier.
6. Possible responses: smoke in the memory of the princess; pyramids that change to volcanoes; Popo's decision to stand on top of the pyramid forever.

The People Could Fly

p. 305 Reading Strategy: Students should underline *people who could fly; slavery; slave ships, magic of flying,* and *dark-skinned.*

p. 305 Reading Check: The people are full of misery because they can't fly any more. They are miserable because they have been enslaved.

p. 305 Reading Check: Some people have the special gift of being able to fly.

p. 306 Literary Analysis: Students should circle the words *call him Toby; standin',* and *Now.*

p. 306 Reading Check: Sarah can't feed her baby because the overseer is watching.

p. 306 Reading Strategy: Possible responses: violence; abuse; treating people and babies badly.

p. 307 Literary Analysis: Students should underline *said so quickly* and *sounded like whispers and sighs.*

p. 307 Reading Check: Possible response: The master wants to kill Toby because Toby is helping slaves escape.

p. 307 Reading Check: The magic words are *buba yali* and *buba tambe.*

p. 308 Literary Analysis: The message is that people should have hope and they will be saved.

p. 308 English Language Development: Students should circle *goodie-bye.*

p. 308 Culture Note: Students' answers will vary based on their native culture. Encourage students to share the stories with the class.

Review and Assess

1. The people lose their wings when they become slaves.

2. Sarah tells Toby she must leave soon because she thought she would die.

3. Toby helps Sarah by chanting a spell and helping her fly.

4. Possible responses include: *say; hollerin',* and *Couldn't believe it, call him Toby; standin', Call her Sarah,* and *Now.*

5. Life was painful and hard. They wanted to be free and they wanted to be safe.

Demeter and Persephone

p. 313 Literary Analysis: The events might describe volcanic eruptions.

p. 313 Reading Strategy: Eros will shoot an arrow and someone will fall in love. Some students may predict that this love will stop the monsters from shaking the earth.

p. 314 Literary Analysis: The Greeks say that people are hit by Eros' arrow and fall in love.

p. 314 Reading Check: Students should underline *Eros shoots an arrow straight into Pluto's heart* and *a young woman gathering flowers.*

p. 314 Reading Check: Persephone is the daughter of Demeter, the goddess of the harvest. Pluto kidnaps Persephone.

p. 315 Literary Analysis: The ancient Greeks believed that natural disasters were caused by the gods.

p. 315 Reading Strategy: Students may predict that Zeus will save Persephone.

p. 315 Vocabulary and Pronunciation: The present form of the verb *sped* is *speed.* The past form of the given words are as follows: *bleed*/bled; *meet*/met; *keep*/kept.

p. 315 Reading Check: tasted food in the realm of the dead.

p. 316 Reading Check: She likes things with fragrance. Jewels have no fragrance.

p. 316 Reading Strategy: Students may predict that Persephone will be very unhappy or that she will die.

p. 316 Literary Analysis: We have winter because Demeter doesn't allow things to grow while her daughter, Persephone, is with Pluto.

Review and Assess

1. Pluto takes Persephone to his kingdom because he is in love with her.

2. The correct answer is C.

3. Zeus solves the problem by asking Hermes to bring Persephone back.

4. When Persephone is on earth, there is spring and summer. When she is in the underworld the earth has fall and winter.

5. The myth of Demeter and Persephone explains the cycle of the seasons.

6. Possible responses: **Persephone:** *Prediction:* Students may have predicted she would die. *Outcome:* She did not die; but she was not completely happy either. **Demeter:** *Prediction:* Students may have predicted that Demeter would get Persephone back. *Outcome:* Demeter was able to get Persephone back for part of the year.

Icarus and Daedalus

p. 321 Reading Check: Students should circle *a wonderful Labyrinth.*

p. 321 Reading Check: It seemed impossible to leave because every ship was guarded.

p. 321 Reading Strategy: Students should say what they think Daedalus will do.

p. 322 Vocabulary and Pronunciation: a pair of shoes; a pair of socks; a pair of gloves.

p. 322 Vocabulary and Pronunciation: It means he was not paying attention to what he heard.

p. 322 Reading Strategy: If he doesn't remember his father's instructions he might be badly hurt or even die.

p. 322 Reading Strategy: The heat of the sun could melt his feathers apart.

p. 323 Culture Note: Ask students to try to name at least one story.

p. 323 Reading Check: Students should underline the following: *The heat of the sun had melted the wax from his wings; the feathers were falling.*

p. 323 Stop to Reflect: Students should say what they would do in the same situation.

Review and Assess

1. He is in Crete.

2. He plans to create wings so he can fly away.

3. He warns him not to fly too low or too high.

4. Icarus drowns at the end of the myth.

5. The myth teaches us the importance of being careful and cautious, and it teaches us to pay attention to others when they are teaching us how to do something that can be dangerous.

6. The following are some clues from the story: His father's instructions "went in at one ear and out by the other." / Icarus forgets all the instructions and soars as high as he can. / His father is way below him.

Answers to Part 2

Burning Out at Nine?

p. 329 Read Fluently: Students should underline three of the following: "He wakes up at 6 every weekday morning," "downs a five minute breakfast," "reports to school at 7:50," "returns home at 3:15," "hits the books from 5 to 9," and "goes to sleep at 10:30."

p. 329 Reading Strategy: The author thinks that children's schedules are too busy. Students should circle "Remember when enjoying life seemed like the point of childhood? Huh!"

p. 330 Vocabulary and Pronunciation: Possible response: a piece of wood cut from a tree; a journal or book

p. 330 Reading Strategy: The use of experts' opinions strengthens the author's argument by giving the impression that what the author says is true.

p. 330 Reading Check: The average child spends 12 hours a week in unstructured play.

p. 331 Reading Informational Materials: The story does not mention the opinions of experts or parents who think that children today have enough leisure time. It also doesn't mention the opinions of those who think that children have too much leisure time.

p. 332 Review and Assess
Check Your Comprehension

1. Children's leisure time is defined as time left over after sleeping, eating, personal hygiene, and attending school or day care.

2. Unstructured play encourages independent thinking and allows children to negotiate relationships with their peers.

3. (a) The amount of time children spend watching television has dropped by 25 percent. (b) The amount of time children spend reading has changed very little.

Applying the Reading Strategy

4. They show mostly negative effects of busy schedules for children.

5. Possible response: Children's busy schedules are having a negative effect on their health and happiness.

Writing Informational Materials

Possible sources of information include the Internet, magazines, newspapers, and interviews.

Golden Girls

p. 334 Reading Strategy: Students may underline any of the following: "the lumps in their throats," "the chills that ran down their spines," "the eye-dampening sight," "high-stepping," "a steadily building roar of oh-oh-ooOOHH!" and the quote by A. J. Mleczko. These words suggest that the author is happy about the victory and can relate to the team's feelings of excitement and emotion.

p. 334 Vocabulary and Pronunciation: Students should circle two of the following: "eye-dampening," "high-stepping," or "empty-net." *Eye-dampening* describes a sight that puts tears in someone's eyes. *High-stepping* describes the way a person moves. *Empty-net* describes the goal.

p. 335 Reading Strategy: Students should circle "(b) admiring." An example that supports the attitude might be the author's description of the "saves, many of them spectacular."

p. 335 Read Fluently: Students should circle the word "grousing"; students should underline the word "gushing."

p. 335 Reading Informational Materials: The quotations support the author's attitude and also add interest because they contain the exact words of real people.

p. 336 Review and Assess
Comprehension Check

1. (a) Her dream was to play on the U.S. national soccer team. (b) She had not received an invitation to try out for the team.

2. This victory could give other female athletes hope for future performances and victories.

Applying the Reading Strategy

3. It suggests that she admires the team members and respects their talent.

4. She thinks that women are up to the challenge of playing "grittier" sports if given the opportunity. She says this in the concluding paragraph of the article.

Writing Informational Materials

Possible response:

1. How did it feel to win the gold medal?

2. What other teams did you have to beat to get to the finals?

3. Do you plan to keep playing hockey?

Memos

p. 338 Vocabulary and Pronunciation:
FR: from; who sent the memo
RE: regarding; what the memo is about
CC: copies; who gets copies of the memo
Encl. Enclosure; what additional paperwork comes with the memo

p. 338 Read Fluently: The deadline is 12/15/00.

p. 338 Reading Informational Materials: The headings come first. The first paragraph contains the most important information. Other details follow. The paragraphs are set up in block style. Each paragraph discusses one thing in direct language. The format works well because the information can be read quickly by employees, and they will know exactly what to do.

p. 339 Review and Assess
Check Your Comprehension

1. They can continue to use their badges for two weeks.

2. They need the badges to enter the building.

Applying the Reading Strategy

3. Answer: John Charles, Facilities Manager
Abbreviation or heading: FR
Answer: 12/1/00
Abbreviation or heading: DATE

Answer: Photo Ids
Abbreviation or heading: RE
Answer: All Employees at Needham Facility
Abbreviation or heading: TO
Answer: Captain Schaeffer, Security Chief;
Don Rolds, USR Facilities Manager; Linda
O'Connell, director of Human Resources
Abbreviation or heading: cc

4. a map to the security office

Writing Informational Materials

Possible response:
TO: All students in Mrs. Johnson's 4th
period English class
FR: John Doe
DATE: 01/31/04
RE: Car Wash
CC: Mrs. Johnson, Principal Greenstone
Encl: Advertising Flier
On March 3 from 1pm to 5pm our class
will hold a car wash at the gas station on
the corner of Elm and Locust. Please bring
a rag and a bucket with you. Post the
enclosed flier in your neighborhood.

A Colony in the Sky

p. 341 Read Fluently:

1. The more we know about the solar
   system's other planets, the better we will
   understand Earth.
2. This will make us safer.

p. 342 Reading Check: Students may choose
three of the following: general size,
presence of water, length of days, or range
of temperatures.

p. 342 Reading Strategy Students should
circle the word "recipe."

p. 343 Reading Strategy: Students may
name two of the following: growing a
garden, creating a wilderness, building a
cathedral, or flying seeds over an ocean to
drop them on a new island.

p. 343 Stop to Reflect: Students may say
that terraforming Mars is a good idea
because it will help us learn more about
Earth. Others may say it is not a good idea
because it is not possible. Answers will
vary, but they should include valid reasons.

p. 343 Reading Informational Materials:
Possible responses:
1. *Discover*
2. *National Geographic*

3. a science magazine
4. a magazine for school children

p. 344 Review and Assess

Check Your Comprehension

1. Mars resembles Earth in its size, presence
   of water, length of day, and range of
   temperatures.
2. "To terraform" means to alter Mars's
   surface to make it able to sustain Earth's
   plants and animals. It would require
   adding nitrogen, oxygen, and water as well
   as importing Earth's life forms. In addition,
   it would take centuries to form.

Applying the Reading Strategy

3. The analogy presents a difficult concept—
   terraforming—by comparing it to a familiar
   concept—cooking. Relating it to a simple
   concept helps readers understand the
   thinking behind the unfamiliar process
   and helps relieve fears of the process.
4. (a) The writer compares the colonization
   of Mars to a giant laboratory or university.
   (b) The items being compared are the
   colonization of Mars and a laboratory/
   university. Both are sites of experiments
   and places of learning.

Writing Informational Materials

Possible responses:
Planting a seed is like burying treasure.
Cutting the grass is like giving the Earth a
haircut.
Healthy eating is like putting the proper
kind of gasoline in your car.

Algal Blooms

p. 346 Reading Textbooks: Possible
response: It is helpful to include a picture
because readers may not know what an
algal bloom is or what it looks like.

p. 346 Reading Check: They found toxins.

p. 347 Reading Textbooks: Students should
underline "the algae that grow rapidly . . .
turn the color of the water red."

p. 347 Read Fluently: Possible response:
When there is an increase in the amount
of nutrients in the water, red tides will
occur more frequently.

p. 347 Vocabulary and Pronunciation: The
word *present* also means "gift."

p. 348 Reading Textbooks: Possible response: If you didn't know the answer to the Check Point question, you could go back and reread the selection in order to find the answer.

p. 348 Reading Informational Materials: The feature is the heading "Integrating Technology." This heading helps readers locate specific information quickly.

p. 349 Review and Assess

Check Your Comprehension

1. Some whales died because they consumed toxic algae and fish.
2. An algal bloom is the rapid growth of a population of algae.

Applying the Reading Strategy

3. An increase in nutrients in the water, an increase in water temperature, and seasonal changes can cause red tides.
4. Technology enables scientists to track how red tides move and to detect increases in ocean temperature.

Using Informational Material

Possible response:

1. This literature textbook is organized into units.
2. The images visually show the subject matter of the selections. They also make the textbook more interesting.
3. This textbook uses headings, subheadings, and checkpoint questions to call out important information.

How Do Rainmakers Make It Rain ?

p. 351 Reading Essays: Possible response: A question can indicate a cause-and-effect relationship. The question in the title of this essay shows that the essay will explore the causes of rain.

p. 351 Read Fluently: Some clouds do not produce rain because the particles of water never grow large enough to fall to the ground as rain.

p. 352 Reading Check: The effect is that pure water in supercooled clouds does not freeze even when its temperature is below the freezing point. Students should circle the following sentence: "But the water can be 10 or 20 degrees below freezing (supercooled) without actually freezing."

p. 352 Reading Strategy:

1. 70 mm guns fire silver iodide particles at supercooled clouds.
2. Explosions spread the silver iodide particles at the right height.
3. Silver iodide helps water particles freeze and grow large.
4. When the particles become heavy enough, they fall to the ground as rain.

p. 352 Reading Informational Materials: The clouds must be supercooled in order to produce increased rainfall.

p. 353 Review and Assess

Check Your Comprehension

1. Clouds are made of tiny particles of water.
2. Small droplets of rain evaporate before they reach the ground.
3. Silver iodide particles have been dropped from aircraft, carried by rockets, fired by guns, or released at ground level so air currents could carry them into the atmosphere.

Applying the Reading Strategy

4. Most students will choose the cause-and-effect relationship in which a single cause triggers a series of events. For instance, firing silver iodide particles at clouds triggers a series of events that result in falling rain.
5. It is important for a writer to choose a cause-and-effect relationship before writing in order to reach a complete under-standing of how events are connected. This knowledge allows the writer to explain these relationships more clearly to an audience.

Writing Informational Materials

Students should choose a historical topic and a type of cause-and-effect organization before writing their essays. A variety of cause-and-effect organizations are valid for historical topics. For example, the suggested topic, the American Revolution, could be represented chronologically as a chain of events. Or, it could be seen as a multitude of causes (the Stamp Act, the lack of representation in English Parliament, etc.)

producing a single effect. Students should consistently apply their chosen organization to their essays.

Signs

p. 355 Reading Signs: The most important information is the name of The National Oregon Trail Center. It is in the biggest and boldest type.

p. 355 Read Fluently: Students should circle "5:00 PM."

p. 355 Reading Strategy: Your purpose might be to find out about special group times and rates. The sign tells you whom to call to get the information you need.

p. 356 Reading Strategy: A hiker might want to know what happened at the site.

p. 356 Reading Informational Materials: First sign
1. hours of operation
2. cost to visit
3. who to contact to set up school trips
Second sign
1. what happened at the site
2. who is buried there

p. 357 Review and Assess
Check Your Comprehension
1. The Trail Center opens at 10:00 A.M.
2. Ormond Alford, his sons William M. Alford and Lorenzo D. Alford, and John W. Cameron, a friend, are buried there.

Applying the Reading Strategy
3. Possible response: When is it open? Are tours available? How much does it cost to visit?
4. The physical arrangement of information about times, the word *tours*, and a list of admission prices would help a visitor find that information.

Writing Informational Materials
Students will probably put the name of the museum in the largest type. Other information should include the hours of operation, the cost of visiting, special arrangements, and special exhibits.

The Eternal Frontier

p. 359 Reading Essays: The author asks, "Where is the frontier now?" The author will support his position that the frontier lies in outer space.

p. 359 Read Fluently: Possible response: By citing statistics and numerical facts, L'Amour supports his position that the new frontier is outer space. He cites statistics to show that Earth is overpopulated and overdeveloped, supporting his position that space exploration is a good idea.

p. 360 Culture Note: Possible responses: People tend to have a curious and pioneering nature. Space exploration can lead to scientific and technological discoveries.

p. 360 Reading Strategy: Possible response: The author's main purpose is to convince readers of the need to explore outer space. Students may underline any of the following: "Mankind is not bound by its atmospheric envelope . . . by any limits at all," "It is our destiny to move out . . . to dare the unknown," "It is our destiny to achieve," "Yet we must not forget . . . did not exist before," or "The computer age has arisen . . . of computing devices."

p. 360 Reading Informational Materials: Possible response: This statement helps readers see L'Amour's point of view: If we do not explore new technologies and advances, we will never move forward or realize our full potential as a society.

p. 361 Review and Assess
Check Your Comprehension
1. L'Amour refers to outer space as the "eternal frontier."
2. He says we need leaders with perspective, "men and women who can take the long view and help to shape the outlines of our future."

Applying the Reading Strategy
3. Students should identify any of the facts and statistics L'Amour uses about past inventions, such as radio, automobiles, television, airplanes, electricity, and paving of roads, to show that humankind has been inventive on Earth and should pursue space exploration.

4. Some students may say that L'Amour achieves his purpose because he uses solid facts to support his point and is convincing. Other students may say he fails to achieve his purpose because he does not refute opposing arguments.

Writing Informational Materials

Tell students to use persuasive techniques such as emotional appeal, facts, and statistics to support their positions. Remind students that their arguments should be convincing and sound.

Walking for Exercise and Pleasure

p. 363 Reading Government: Publications' Headings break up the text into more manageable sections; they give clues to the information in each section so that people can quickly find what they are looking for.

p. 363 Read Fluently: Students should circle "39.5%." This number represents the group of people that had the highest percentage of regular walkers: men 65 years of age or older.

p. 363 Stop to Reflect: Possible responses: People walk for pleasure, to relieve tension, for exercise, to get somewhere, or to be alone. Students may say that their parents or grandparents walk. They should give reasons.

p. 364 Reading Strategy: Students should choose four of the following:
1. Walking can improve the body's ability to consume oxygen.
2. It lowers a person's resting heart rate.
3. It reduces blood pressure.
4. It increases the efficiency of the heart and lungs.
5. It burns calories.

p. 364 Reading Check: Walking and running burn approximately the same amount of calories per mile. Running burns calories faster. Students should circle "Briskly walking one mile in 15 minutes burns just about the same number of calories as jogging an equal distance in 8 1/2 minutes."

p. 364 Vocabulary and Pronunciation: Students should circle "qualities," "common," "activities," and "unique."

p. 365 Reading Check:
1. It doesn't cost anything.
2. You can do it almost anytime and anywhere.
3. Almost anyone can do it.

p. 365 Reading Strategy: They are causes because they explain *why* walking is so popular.

p. 365 Reading Informational Materials: Students might point out the headings within the document, the bulleted list, the short paragraphs, or the clear, direct language.

p. 366 Review and Assess

Check Your Comprehension

1. Approximately one-half of Americans claim to exercise regularly.
2. Characteristics of an efficient walking style include holding the head erect, keeping the back straight and the abdomen flat, pointing the toes straight ahead, swinging the arms loosely at the sides, landing on the heel of the foot and rolling forward, taking long and easy strides, leaning forward when walking rapidly or walking up or down hills, and breathing deeply.

Applying the Reading Strategy

3. You should invest in a comfortable pair of shoes, walk with good posture and form, and walk regularly.
4. If you experience dizziness, nausea, or pain, you should slow down or stop walking.

Using Informational Materials

Students' paragraphs should reflect the information they learned in the publication. Remind students to describe several specific advantages of walking. Tell students that their persuasive arguments should be backed up with facts.

The Iceman

p. 368 Reading Primary Research: Lessem's main point is to describe Ötzi, the frozen man, and the objects found with him. Lessem explains that these objects show what Ötzi's life and times were like.

p. 368 Reading Check: Students should circle "Ötzi may have been a shepherd . . . in search of messages from gods."

p. 369 Reading Strategy: Possible response: The bow and arrow found with Ötzi indicate that he was an experienced hunter. Based on the fact there was a forest on the other side of the mountain, it is possible that Ötzi had planned to go hunting.

p. 369 Read Fluently: Students should circle "hard flints" and "fine ax."

p. 369 Reading Primary Research: Students should note that the author bases his conclusion on the discovery of the flint and felt strips.

p. 370 Reading Strategy: Possible response: Ötzi died from the cold and snow. It took 5,000 years for his body to be discovered. Ötzi's belongings help people to better understand life during the Copper Age.

p. 370 Reading Informational Materials: Most students will probably agree that presenting evidence in the form of a story is very useful. It helps to put the evidence into context so that readers have a better understanding of the facts.

p. 371 Review and Assess

Check Your Comprehension

1. Ötzi's physical build indicates his strength, and his tattoos suggest that he may have been regarded as brave.

2. At such a high altitude, there were no twigs to burn.

3. If they searched, they would have found only a blanket of snow.

Applying the Reading Strategy

4. He had a finely crafted bow and arrows, as well as an ax.

5. Possible response: He froze to death because he could not build a fire. Because he was frozen, his body was preserved.

Using Informational Materials

Possible response: Primary research articles focus on information that has been acquired first-hand. Their purpose is to share new and unpublished information. The purpose of encyclopedias, however, is to categorize and relate all known information. Articles found in encyclopedias are based on information found in other articles and on primary research articles.

Let the Reader Beware

p. 378 Reading Guidelines: The title "Let the Reader Beware" refers to information on the Internet. The author is saying that information on the Internet frequently lacks credibility.

p. 378 Reading Strategy: The heading is a summary of the main idea of the paragraphs below it. Each heading is a tip for evaluating information on the Internet.

p. 379 Stop to Reflect: Students should indicate that the second meaning of *home page* is appropriate because the text refers to biographical information.

p. 379 Vocabulary and Pronunciation: This word is appropriate because the author is asking readers to think about reasons that may not be apparent at first. Through analysis, readers are removing the agenda from where it is buried (in the earth) and exposing it to the light of knowledge and understanding.

p. 379 Reading Guidelines: Students should underline sentences that include the following phrases: "current information is usually more valid and useful than older material" and "check out some of its links."

p. 380 Reading Check: Students should circle the sentence "Ideally, you should confirm the information with at least two other sources." It is especially important to triangulate data if it runs counter to your understanding or if you are using the information for an important decision.

p. 380 Reading Informational Materials: It is useful to have boxes in guidelines in order to call readers' attention to information that is particularly useful.

p. 381 Review and Assess

Check Your Comprehension

1. Possible response: One danger is that the source of the information could be inaccurate or biased.

2. Information on the Internet can be verified by checking other reputable Web sites or by consulting print sources. The reader can also check the credentials of the author or organization who is posting the information on the Internet.

Applying the Reading Strategy

3. The introduction explains the purpose of the guidelines.

4. The numbered points summarize the main ideas and make the information easy to find.

5. The format of these guidelines does not follow a strict chronological order. Guidelines on how to access the Internet would have to follow a chronological, step-by-step order to be useful.

Using Informational Materials

Possible responses:

1. Guidelines for a research report assignment

2. Guidelines for how to handle an emergency situation

1. Guidelines for how to operate office equipment

2. Guidelines for taking sick days and vacation days

The Bill of Rights

p. 383 Reading Public Documents: Possible response: A document written today would be typed, not handwritten. It would be on regular white paper, not parchment paper.

p. 384 Reading Strategy: Check students' definitions of words.

p. 384 Read Fluently: Possible response: The accused has the right to a speedy trial with an impartial jury. The accused also has the right to be informed of his or her crime and to be represented by a lawyer.

p. 385 Reading Informational Materials: Direct wording leaves less room for misinterpretation or misunderstanding of the laws.

p. 386 Review and Assess

Check Your Comprehension

1. The First Amendment protects freedom of religion, speech, and the press.

2. The state or the people hold powers that the Constitution does not specifically give to the United States, according to the Tenth Amendment.

Applying the Reading Strategy

3. Students should summarize each amendment, as in the chart on p. 382.

4. Students should identify the unfamiliar words and look them up in a dictionary.

Writing Informational Materials

Students' revisions should indicate a clear understanding of the amendment and should be written in their own words.

Pandas

p. 388 Reading Research Reports: The main idea of this report is that the giant panda is a rare and special animal.

p. 388 Read Fluently: Students should circle "the World Wildlife Fund (WWF)."

p. 389 Reading Strategy: Possible response: To what other animals are pandas related? Which zoos have pandas? How can I help the pandas?

p. 389 Stop to Reflect: Possible response:
1. Giant pandas can only live in cool bamboo forests.
2. Pandas do not have many babies.

p. 390 Vocabulary and Pronunciation: Students should circle the words "against" and "smuggle." They should underline the word "manage."

p. 390 Reading Check: Possible response: Main Idea: The Chinese people and international conservation organizations are working hard to protect pandas. Supporting Detail: There are currently thirteen special panda reserves where some 800 pandas are living in safety.

p. 391 Reading Informational Materials: Authors use more than one source to get as much support for their ideas as they can and to provide varied information.

p. 392 Review and Assess

Check Your Comprehension

1. Pandas need to live in cool, damp places with plenty of bamboo.

2. Pandas eat mostly bamboo, but they also eat fish, rats, bulbs, tree bark, roots, and grasses.

Applying the Reading Strategy

3. Students might list the following questions: Why are pandas so rare? Which zoos house pandas? These questions are likely to occur to readers because they specifically relate to information in the first paragraph.

4. Students might ask the following: Who funds the reserves? Where are the reserves located? These are logical questions that relate to information in the text.

Writing Informational Materials

Possible response:
Detail: Pandas in zoos
Questions: What special environments are built for the pandas?
Where are the zoos that have pandas?
What do the pandas eat?
Sources: Web sites for different zoos
Encyclopedia
Nature or science magazines

A Christmas Carol

p. 394 Reading Literary Criticism: The criticism is written for television viewers. The subtitle "Picks & Pans: Television" indicates that it is written for television viewers.

p. 394 Read Fluently: Students should circle "But TNT's *Carol* would be worth watching if only for the lead performance of Patrick Stewart."

p. 394 Reading Strategy: The statement "Old story well told" indicates a positive response.

p. 395 Reading Literary Criticism: Possible responses: Popular actors attract audiences, so readers who recognize a favorite actor's name might watch the presentation simply to see that actor perform. The list also helps viewers to identify the characters and actors in the production.

p. 395 Read Fluently: Students should circle "Handsome, wholesome, and finely tuned, the cable web's take on Charles Dickens's 1843 masterwork is TV at its classiest."

p. 396 Vocabulary and Pronunciation: The word *often* begins with the letters *o-f-t. Oft-told tales* means "Tales that have been told many times."

p. 396 Stop to Reflect: Possible responses: Some students will say the summary is detailed enough for an understanding of the review because the nature of a review is to summarize. However, others may say the summary does not give them enough

information and phrases such as "Scrooge's hum gets de-bugged" are vague and confusing.

p. 396 Reading Check: Joel Gray is Christmas Past. Desmond Barrit is Christmas Present. Tim Potter is Christmas Future.

p. 397 Reading Literary Criticism: Students should circle "The supporting actors are also first-rate."

p. 397 Reading Strategy: The critic says the strongest aspect of the performance is its "overall execution." The critic also says that Robert Halmi Sr.'s visuals are "the best so far" and that "the restrained magic is very effective."

p. 398 Reading Check: Students should circle *The Oakland Press.*

p. 398 Stop to Reflect: Students should circle the letter *b.*

p. 399 Reading Strategy: He says the set design is "enormous and gorgeous."

p. 399 Stop to Reflect: Possible response: The actors whom the reviewer mentions by name are the "standouts," or leading performers.

p. 400 Reading Strategy: Students should underline any two of the following: "debut," "in perfect keeping with Wicks's toned-down production," "not quite as charismatic a miser as Coleman," "a much darker, even scarier Scrooge," and "that much more affecting."

p. 400 Reading Informational Materials: Possible response: Such literary criticisms might be found in magazines, newspapers, books, entertainment journals, and Web sites.

p. 401 Review and Assess
Check Your Comprehension

1. The *People Weekly* critic is tired of such adaptations. The critic writes, "The Charles Dickens classic has been adapted nearly to death."

2. The Meadow Brook Theatre has produced the play many times. Readers know this because the reviewer says the theatre is "still producing" the play, and the reviewer compares the current production to past productions at the theatre.

Applying the Reading Strategy

3. Possible response: "The ex-skipper of *Star Trek: The Next Generation* ... consistently interesting and intelligent."

4. Possible response: *People Weekly*—"So you muttered 'humbug' when you spied yet another version of *A Christmas Carol* on the TV schedule."; *Variety*—"Oft-told tales are difficult to pull off. . . ."; *The Oakland Press*—"Director Debra Wicks has tinkered . . . just enough to make the old holiday fruitcake seem fresh."

Writing Informational Materials

Students' paragraphs should contain comparisons and contrasts of the critics' reviews of setting, plot, characterization, and performance. The paragraphs should also explain which review best helped them to visualize the productions. Students should support their opinions with examples from the reviews.

Making Fantasy Real

p. 403 Reading Responses to Literature: The birth and death dates might be included to provide background information about the author and to provide the context of the historical period during which the author lived.

p. 403 Read Fluently: Students should circle two of the following: "Little Claus and Big Claus," "The Princess and the Pea," and "The Emperor's New Clothes."

p. 404 Reading Strategy: The writer says that in spite of the physical agony of the mermaid, the reader still feels that the prince is worth dying for.

p. 404 Reading Response to Literature: Possible response: You learn that Anderson believed that there is beauty in all creatures. The writer makes a connection between Anderson's own life and that of the swan in "The Ugly Duckling."

p. 404 Reading Informational Materials: Possible response: Some students may say that reading a response first is helpful because it provides background and context for the literary work. Others may say that a response might give away plot details and therefore spoil the fun of reading a literary work.

p. 405 Review and Assess
Check Your Comprehension

1. Anderson first published a travel diary.

2. Anderson added motivation and believability to the characters.

Applying the Reading Strategy

3. The writer believes that "The Ugly Duckling" is symbolic of Anderson's life.

4. The writer quotes a description from "The Steadfast Tin Soldier" to support her belief.

Writing Informational Materials

Students should answer each of the questions as thoroughly as possible. Their responses should show a clear understanding of the elements of a response to literature.

How to Use Your New Alarm Chronograph Timer

p. 407 Reading Directions: Studying a diagram is useful because it helps people familiarize themselves with the parts of a device before they learn how to operate it.

p. 407 Stop to Reflect: The list of features tells what functions the device is able to perform. In this case, the list of features tells you that you can use the watch to set an alarm or to time an event.

p. 407 Reading Strategy: Possible response: To begin any operation—whether setting the time or using the stopwatch—you need to be able to switch to the appropriate function, or mode.

p. 408 Reading Check: Students should circle the line "Turn to set function to ALARM."

p. 408 Reading Strategy: Possible response: The best way to explain would be to demonstrate each of the steps for setting the alarm, and then to have the person set the alarm himself or herself.

p. 408 Vocabulary and Pronunciation: Possible response: Another meaning of operation is "surgery."

p. 409 Reading Informational Materials: You would use the boldface headings to skip to the section with the directions for the countdown timer.

p. 410 Review and Assess

Check Your Comprehension

5. You can set the timer 12 hours ahead.

6. To stop the alarm from sounding, press Button A or B.

Apply the Reading Strategy

7. The alarm chronograph timer has an analog display. It also has two buttons on the left side and a crown on the right side to control its functions.

8. Use the chronograph feature for timing someone who is running a 200-meter dash.

9. Possible response: Set the function to "Timer," and then set the desired time by pressing Button B. To start and stop the timer, press Button A. Press Button B to reset the timer.

Writing Informational Materials

Students should choose a device, and then describe how to use two separate functions in step-by-step format. For example, a student might describe how to tune in a radio station and adjust the bass level on a stereo.

Bat Attacks?

p. 412 Reading Strategy: The main point of comparison is between wooden bats and aluminum bats.

p. 412 Read Fluently: Some energy is lost when the ball compresses against the bat. The resulting friction releases energy as heat.

p. 412 Reading Strategy: Students should underline all sentences in the paragraph except the final sentence. The author's main point is that baseball players using aluminum bats hit balls farther than players using wooden bats.

p. 413 Culture Note: A professional athlete is paid a salary to play a particular sport; an amateur athlete is not.

p. 413 Reading Informational Materials: The author returns to his point that the use of aluminum bats could lead to an increase in injuries.

p. 414 Review and Assess

Check Your Comprehension

1. The author believes that aluminum bats are more dangerous because balls hit with aluminum bats tend to fly faster and farther than those hit with wooden bats. She fears the use of aluminum bats could lead to an increase in injuries.

2. Aluminum bats compress more because they are hollow inside.

Applying the Reading Strategy

3. The main point of the essay is that aluminum bats cause baseballs to fly faster and farther than wooden bats.

4. Possible responses: Many students will think the author convincingly explains why balls hit with aluminum bats travel faster and farther. Some students will dispute her point that this could lead to more injuries by pointing to the lack of evidence that this has actually taken place.

Writing Informational Materials

Students should choose a subject and write a clear, coherent essay that points out three key similarities and differences. For example, a comparison of two sports might focus on necessary skills, equipment, and physical demands on players.

Tenochtitlan: Inside the Aztec Capital

p. 416 Reading Strategy: Possible response: Heads break up the text and help you find information on specific topics. The words in a head describe what that section is about.

p. 416 Stop to Reflect: Students might say the city map is similar to modern maps because it shows streets and waterways. They might also note that the city map is different because it lacks street names and because it shows buildings and other physical qualities of the city.

p. 416 Read Fluently: Students should circle two of the following: "They built three causeways . . . to link the city with the mainland," "These were raised roads . . . supported on wooden pillars," "Parts of the causeways were bridges," "These bridges . . . prevented enemies from getting to the city," or "Fresh water was brought . . . along stone aqueducts."

p. 417 Stop to Reflect: Possible response: Tenochtitlan was a large city of one-story stone houses with flat roofs. It contained two temples on one side of the center square and the king's palace on the other side. The city was surrounded by water.

p. 417 Reading Social Studies Articles: Possible response: The Aztecs depended on corn and worshiped many gods and goddesses who were in charge of corn.

p. 418 Stop to Reflect: Possible response: The Aztecs were proficient stoneworkers and efficient architects.

p. 418 Reading Strategy: Students should underline "they think it may have been between one third . . . of the population," "The rest were nobility, craftspeople, and others," "Each chinampa . . . food for one family," and "Most people . . . depended on food from outside the city."

p. 418 Read Fluently: They got their food from farms outside the city.

p. 419 Vocabulary and Pronunciation: Students should circle "(b) far from the center."

p. 420 Review and Assess

Check Your Comprehension

1. The city was set in the middle of a lake and swampland.
2. The wealthy lived in the center of the city. The poor lived in the outskirts on the chinampas.

Applying the Reading Strategy

3. The Aztecs used stone and wattle-and-daub.
4. The Aztecs slept on reed mats on dirt floors. They had cooking fires, but no chimneys or windows, so the houses were dark and smoky. They used clay pots and utensils and had graters, grinders, and storage containers.
5. Students should list "corn" and one of the following: tomatoes, beans, chili peppers, prickly pears, maguey cactus, and cacao.

Using Informational Materials

Possible response: 1. People might consult a social studies text to find out about a place that they would like to visit. 2. Another reason might be to learn about the political situations in other countries.

Moving Mountains

p. 422 Reading Strategy: Students should circle the word "erosion." Students should underline "The Himalayas are gradually losing mass" and "the loss of mass is affecting the Himalayas' position on Earth's surface."

p. 422 Reading Check: The Himalayas are the highest mountains in the world.

p. 422 Vocabulary and Pronunciation: 1. *block*: /k/ sound 2. *centimeters*: /s/ sound

p. 423 Read Fluently: Possible response: The numbering shows which step comes first and helps readers to follow the steps in the correct order.

p. 423 Reading Informational Materials: After completing the experiment, readers have the information they need to understand the effects of erosion.

p. 424 Review and Assess

Check Your Comprehension

1. Erosion is causing the Himalayas to lose their mass and shift their position on Earth.
2. Earth's crust is its rigid, outer layer that floats on a layer of molten rock.
3. The essay instructs you to do a demonstration to understand the effect of erosion.

Applying the Reading Strategy

4. Possible response: The water level will change.
5. Possible response: The experiment visually shows the causes and effects of erosion.

Writing Informational Materials

Students should give clear, step-by-step instructions, including a list of materials needed to accomplish the task.